AMERICA BY THE NUMBERS

a high proportion of
Korean Americans are
self-employed   the high-school dropout rate
Boomers are over   for whites was 9%, versus 17% for
25% more likely than   African Americans, and 35% for Latinos
members of other
generations to be   over 65% of all immigrants to the
active in community   US resided in just 10 of the nation
organizations   almost 300 metropolitan areas

over 53% of Generation   the poorest 20
Xers report "being bored"   of households
in the past week   had an average
income of$9,22

over 75%   metropolitan drivers spend
of women   about 40 hours every year
refuse   sitting in stopped traffic
to call
themselves   11% of Gen X singles
feminist   their own houses in 1

Greater Los
Angeles now   During 1998, 660,447 legal
houses 1 out   immigrants, 44,829 refugees,
of 5 Latinos in   and an estimated 275,000
the U.S.   illegal immigrants entered
the United States   50% of first m
will end
divorc

AMERICA
BY THE
NUMBERS

A Field Guide
to the U.S. Population

William H. Frey,

Bill Abresch, and

Jonathan Yeasting

Written in collaboration with
Social Science Data Analysis Network associates:
David Livshiz, Regan Smith, Caitlin Cain,
Eric Kessell, Michelle Johnson,
and Joshua Hill

THE NEW PRESS, NEW YORK

Published in the United States by The New Press, New York, 2001
Distributed by W. W. Norton & Company, Inc., New York

LIBRARY OF CONGRESS CATALOGING-IN-PUBLICATION DATA
Frey, William H.
   America by the numbers: a field guide to the U.S. population / William
H. Frey, Bill Abresch, and Jonathan Yeasting.
      p. cm.
   ISBN 1-56584-641-9 (pbk.)
   1. United States—Population—Statistics. I. Abresch, Bill. II. Yeasting,
Jonathan. III. Title

HA214 .F74 2001
304.6'0973—dc21   00–068122

The New Press was established in 1990 as a not-for-profit alternative to the
large, commercial publishing houses currently dominating the book publishing
industry. The New Press operates in the public interest rather than for private
gain, and is committed to publishing, in innovative ways, works of educational,
cultural, and community value that are often deemed insufficiently profitable.

The New Press, 450 West 41st Street, 6th floor, New York, NY 10036
www.thenewpress.com

Book design by Lovedog Studio

Printed in Canada.

2 4 6 8 10 9 7 5 3 1

CONTENTS

3. PEOPLES: Race, Ethnicity, and Identity

4. IMMIGRANTS: Crossing Borders

5. MOVERS: Mixing and Division within America's Borders

6. CLASSES: Wealth and Poverty

7. WORKERS: Labor's Continuing Necessity

8. FAMILIES: Renegotiating Norms

9. STUDENTS: Schoolbooks and Skills

10. THE ELDERLY: Age and the Graying of America

11. THE HEALTHY: Illness and Well-Being

12. CRIMINALS: Violence and Confinement

13. VOTERS: The Demography of Democracy

ACKNOWLEDGMENTS

This book was a collective effort of the authors and the associates of the Social Science Data Analysis Network (SSDAN). SSDAN is a university-based organization that creates demographic media, such as user manuals, web sites, and hands-on classroom materials. The project's goal is to make information on social and demographic trends, based on census data and other social surveys, lively, engaging, and accessible to a broad audience of educators, policymakers, and informed citizens. An overview of the project can be found on its web site: http://www.ssdan.net.

SSDAN is directed by Dr. William H. Frey at the Population Studies Center of the University of Michigan and involves a network of student and staff associates affiliated with the university. The authors are especially appreciative of the contributions by those SSDAN associates who researched and drafted various parts of the book: David Livshiz, Regan Smith, Caitlin Cain, Eric Kessell, and Michelle Johnson. Joshua Hill developed our graphic presentation and design ideas. Finally, we wish to thank our editors at the New Press, Andy Hsiao and Ellen Reeves, whose encouragement, guidance, and assistance made this project an enjoyable experience for all of us.

WILLIAM H. FREY
BILL ABRESCH
JONATHAN YEASTING

IS DEMOGRAPHY DESTINY?

The phrase "demography is destiny" may overstate the importance of America's demographic history and makeup for our collective future. But there is no question that America's most burning issues and heated policy debates are impacted by baby booms and busts, immigration and exploding diversity, an aging population, the changing roles of women and families, the sharp divisions between cities and suburban sprawl.

One need only look at the daily headlines to find examples ranging from debates over "family values" to the potential insolvency of our Social Security trust fund, from affirmative action to the failures and successes of welfare reform. All of these issues, and the policies that they shape, are directly related to demographic dynamics that are playing out across every part of our national landscape.

Few would disagree that to understand today's policy debates and political conflicts requires a firm knowledge of basic economic principles and of America's political culture. We make the case that it is just as important for an informed citizenry to be conversant with the key social and demographic trends that are reshaping American society in the twenty-first century.

The dramatic changes revealed by the 2000 census have whetted America's appetite for such information. But there has been no easy-to-read handbook with information on a broad array of population-related topics arranged in a "one-stop shopping" format. The publications and web sites of government agencies contain hundreds of dry tables and pages of text that often obfuscate as much as they enlighten. At the other extreme are the glossy and superficial reports disseminated by policy advocates and corporate marketers, tailored to not-so-hidden agendas and sales pitches.

America by the Numbers: A Field Guide to the U.S. Population begins with the conviction that conventionally reported data, once wrested from the hands of bureaucrats, advocates, and marketers, can reveal important social insights. Many of the ways we view American society are fast becoming outmoded. Examining a wide array of social trends and adopting fresh perspectives on old statistics, *America by the Numbers* maps this new terrain by questioning conventional wisdom and reporting the bad news as well as the good.

Why do we know so much more about poor people than millionaires? Is the nuclear family really in meltdown? Are partisans of the "New Economy" playing fast and easy with occupational numbers? Who are the "best cities in America" best for? Questions like these are not addressed in standard social almanacs or statistical yearbooks.

In *America by the Numbers* we resist the temptation to blindly apply old categories to new realities. At the same time, we ground our often provocative questions in objective information and cold, hard statistics. We have attempted to offer a lively, engaging, and sometimes troubling picture of where the nation's population is headed as we tread onward into the new century.

AMERICA BY THE NUMBERS

GENERATIONS

Popular Vanguards

Few demographic developments so capture the popular imagination as the coming of age of a new generation. A scattering of infants who enter the world sharing little but a vague proximity in date of birth is assigned a label meant to capture their personalities, values, buying habits, and political predilections. Generations are amorphous nations with many honorary citizens and not a few reluctant hostages to fate. Yet, these babies grow up together in a common world, learn in the same classrooms, fight the same wars, and prosper or struggle in the same economy. Together, they create new forms of popular culture and transform America's values. Indeed, shifts in attitudes—toward race, gender roles, the place of the family—are seldom a matter of individuals changing their minds, but of the young replacing the old, so that values truly are a matter of life and death. As a generation emerges, it quickly becomes a subject for speculation and manipulation. All are aware that with its members rests America's future. Politicians appeal to its interests, attempting to pit it against other generations. Marketers try to sell it a style. Journalists play the naming game—is it Generation Y, Next, Net, or what?

Population Growth: Demography Is Destiny

The facts: In 1900, the U.S. population was about 76 million. In 2000, it was 281 million. By the year 2060, it is projected to be somewhere between 311 million and 643 million.

Prior to the twentieth century, the United States' explosive population growth—driven in large part by immigration—helped push the frontier across North America. After a lull that stretched through the Great Depression and the Second World War, the population surged with the postwar Baby Boom; and with the repeal of the quota system in 1965, immigration once again began to play a major role in the growth of the U.S. population. Between 1990 and 2000, at least a third of the population growth was the result of immigration.

By the late twentieth century, native-born Americans were having far fewer children. By the 1970s, the birth rate had fallen enough so that the population would have begun to decline if death rates had not also fallen and immigration increased. This effect was particularly pronounced in the white population, but African Americans experienced a decline in birth rate as well. At the beginning of the twenty-first century, population growth is fueled primarily by immigrants and their children. Families in the developing nations from which many immigrants come are often much larger than in the United States. Traditional ways of life are seldom abandoned upon crossing a border. Thus, new residents increase not only the total numbers but also the fertility rate of the total population.

Tangible concerns about people's lives can easily get lost in the flurry of digits, but the extent to which a nation's fortunes are determined by population growth or decline is difficult to discern only because the effects are so pervasive. It is not surprising, then, that pundits and policymakers vacillate between the fear of falling behind in an imagined "people race" against the world's great powers and the fear of outstripping the natural resources needed to support hundreds of millions and counting.

U.S. POPULATION GROWTH IN THE TWENTIETH CENTURY

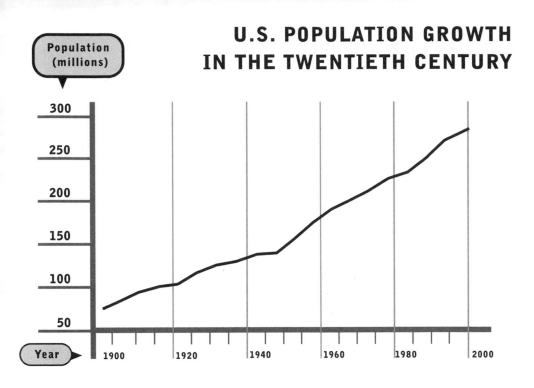

POPULATION PROJECTIONS FOR THE YEAR 2050

Based on differing rates of future immigration

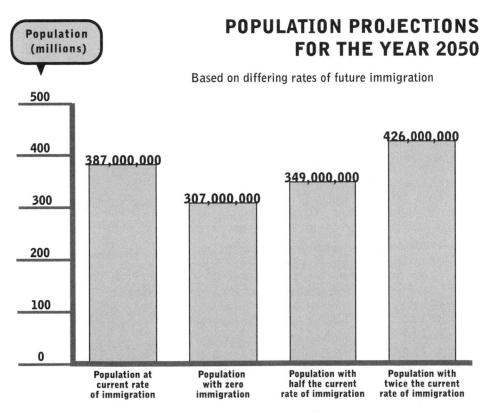

POPULATION STRUCTURE, 2000

Each horizontal bar represents the number of people
of a particular age and sex. The Baby Boom is clearly
visible in the central bulge.

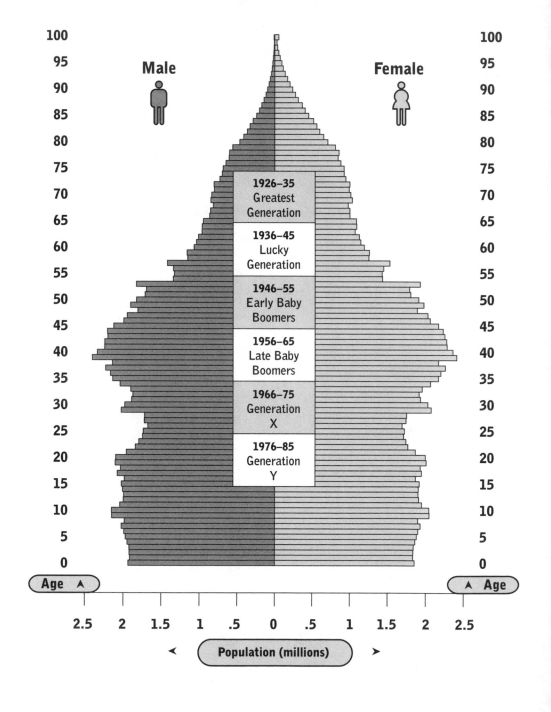

The Architecture
of Population

Populations are produced by birth and death. As simple as this sounds, the fundamental variables of fertility and mortality describe an intricate architecture.

If a population's structure is "bottom-heavy" with children, as the United States' was in the 1950s, it immediately faces a burden of education and child care. Some years later, it benefits from a burgeoning labor force more than large enough to take care of its elders. Finally, the large elderly population burdens the society that needs to support it. These fluctuations in the fertility rate—along with those in rates of mortality and immigration—give a population the intricate structure that fascinates sociologists and plagues policy makers.

1.3 The Greatest Generation

The mythology of the Greatest Generation—for demographic purposes, those born between 1926 and 1935—has had a stern grip on America's national psyche for over half a century. The Greats outlasted the Depression, helped secure victory in World War II, and championed the postwar economic boom. For better or worse, the practices and beliefs the Greats followed in the postwar decades have become established as central "American values": getting married early, having kids, moving to the suburbs (or, perhaps more accurately, inventing the suburbs) to raise them, sending father off to work in industry, and keeping mother at home to care for the children. It is perhaps not surprising, then, that as the Greats age they retain their values: 67.8 percent do not think a woman should be able to obtain an abortion if she wants it for any reason, compared with 54.1 percent of the population as a whole. Only 4.1 percent strongly approve of couples moving in together before marriage, while 76.9 percent think that everyone can benefit from a traditional family. In pre-Viagra 1996, only 12.9 percent had seen an X-rated movie in the past year, compared to 28.5 percent of the general population. This cohort is the most patriotic: while 37 percent of Americans strongly agree that America is a better country than most, that position is taken by 54 percent of Greats.

VETERAN STATUS OF MALES BY GENERATION

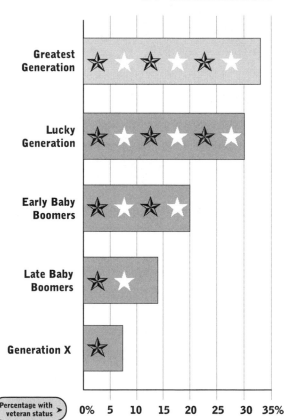

Greatest Generation

Lucky Generation

Early Baby Boomers

Late Baby Boomers

Generation X

Percentage with veteran status

0% 5 10 15 20 25 30 35%

The Lucky Generation

The Lucky Generation was, well, lucky. Born between 1936 and 1945, these pre-Boomers were too young to risk their lives in the Second World War and then came of age in a time of great consumer confidence and national pride. Although the threat of nuclear war hung over them in the days of the Iron Curtain, they entered the job market during a two-decade binge of rising productivity and living standards.

They were the kids with money who introduced the world to consumer society. A numerically small generation following the Depression, they experienced little competition for well-paying jobs, inexpensive housing, and slots in the expanding system of higher education. In a way, the Luckies were the lull before the Boomer storm.

Buoyed by the prosperous postwar economy, the Luckies married young—in 1956, the median age at first marriage was twenty—and proceeded to give birth to Boomers. The Lucky Generation's largest contribution, demographically speaking, has been their progeny.

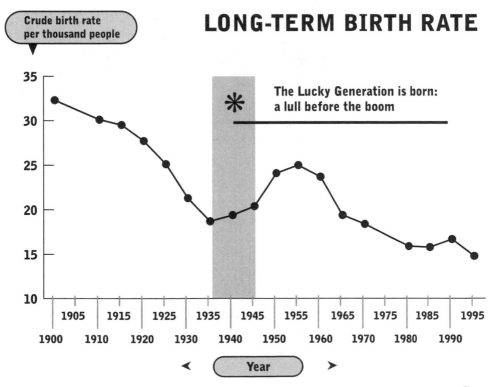

Crude birth rate per thousand people

LONG-TERM BIRTH RATE

The Lucky Generation is born: a lull before the boom

Year

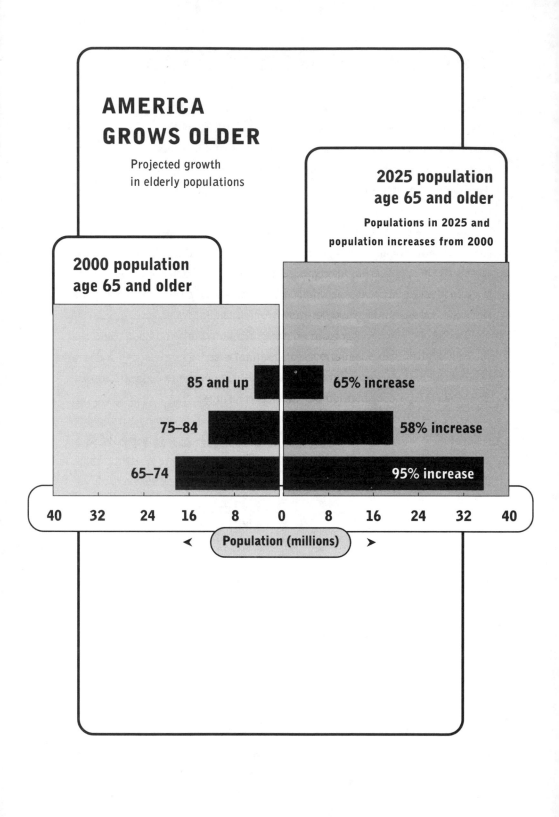

AMERICA GROWS OLDER

Projected growth
in elderly populations

**2000 population
age 65 and older**

**2025 population
age 65 and older**

Populations in 2025 and
population increases from 2000

85 and up — 65% increase

75–84 — 58% increase

65–74 — 95% increase

| 40 | 32 | 24 | 16 | 8 | 0 | 8 | 16 | 24 | 32 | 40 |

◄ **Population (millions)** ►

The Baby Boom's Demography: Strength in Numbers?

About one of every four Americans is a Baby Boomer. Born between 1946 and 1965, this group dwarfs in number their parents' and childrens' generations alike.

Their numbers made the Boomers the most influential cultural class in the twentieth century. As they age, their reputation for activism that emerged in the 1960s has held true even as their means have matured. Not only are Baby Boomers over 25 percent more likely than members of other generations to be active in community organizations; they are also more likely than other generations to be active for causes that Americans tend to associate with Generations X or Y—the environment and women's rights. Yet not every Boomer was a Freedom Rider, a Woodstock attendee, or a peace protester. Indeed, the Boomers helped found neoconservatism, and were the key electoral target for the 1994 Republican takeover of the Congress.

But size has not been an unmitigated blessing for the Boomers. They were educated in large classes, and while the labor force expanded immensely, many were left unemployed. By the late 1970s, the early Boomers were driving up housing costs to the point where the later Boomers were hard pressed to afford the homeownership their parents had enjoyed. An inability to afford children and the cultural shifts of sexual revolution persuaded Boomers to marry later and have fewer children.

By the late 1990s, most early Baby Boomers had reached the pinnacles of their careers, seen their children leave for college, and were contemplating retirement. The wealthier of these new empty nesters have become a key market for second houses, luxury automobiles, and other high-ticket items. In a few years, however, the Boomers' clout may be transformed into an economic drain, as they age and increasingly require social services.

Generation X

By the early 1990s, cultural historians had termed those born between 1966 and 1975 Generation X, because they were an unknown quantity to marketers and politicians. Though perhaps a bit distrusted, "X" is probably more palatable to this cohort than the alternatives that have been suggested—the Slackers or the Apathy Generation. Generation X was born in time to witness Nixon resigning, has always lived with environmental degradation, was first exposed to music through disco, and grew up during the "me first" culture of the 1980s. As they grew, they became a key constituency of most environmental groups and created and supported music like grunge and "riot grrl" hardcore.

While doubtless some Gen Xers are apathetic, cynical, or even slackers (over 53 percent do report "being bored" in the past week, compared to 29 percent of Boomers), many are progressive, optimistic, and highly motivated. Over 58 percent believe one should follow one's conscience even if it means breaking the law, while 61.6 percent think that everyone can benefit from a traditional family—a smaller proportion than older cohorts, but still substantial. And many have good reason to feel disenchanted with a system, typified by Great and Boomer authority, that left this generation worse off than its parents. Although their average annual income after taxes is $38,430, single Gen Xers are worse off by every economic measure, excepting choices of entertainment, than either early or late single Boomers at the same point in their lives. Those in their mid twenties in 1995 made less money, consumed fewer luxury goods, and ate at restaurants less often than those in their mid twenties in 1975 or 1985. That 11 percent of Gen X singles owned their own houses in 1995 versus 4 percent of Boomer singles in 1975 seems as much a shift in housing patterns as it is the effect of Boomer legacy—the condominium.

Gen Xers are substantially more accepting of a variety of family forms. Of all living generations, they are the most likely to approve of couples living together before marriage, with only 25.6 percent opposing cohabitation. And only 29.9 percent of white Gen Xers oppose a relative marrying interracially, a much lower percentage than older Americans.

ACCEPTING GAYNESS: A GENERATIONAL NORM

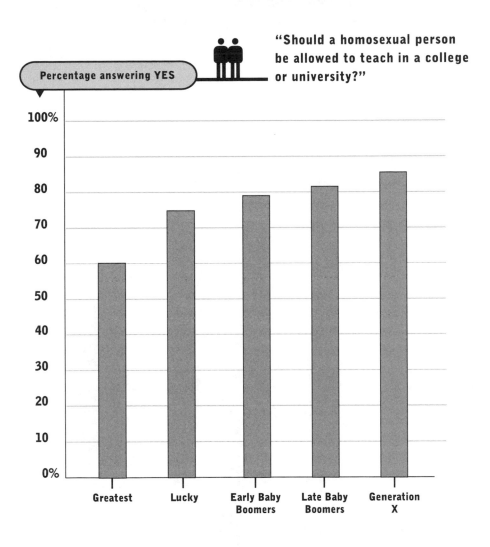

Percentage answering YES

"Should a homosexual person be allowed to teach in a college or university?"

WHAT DO KIDS USE COMPUTERS FOR?, 1997

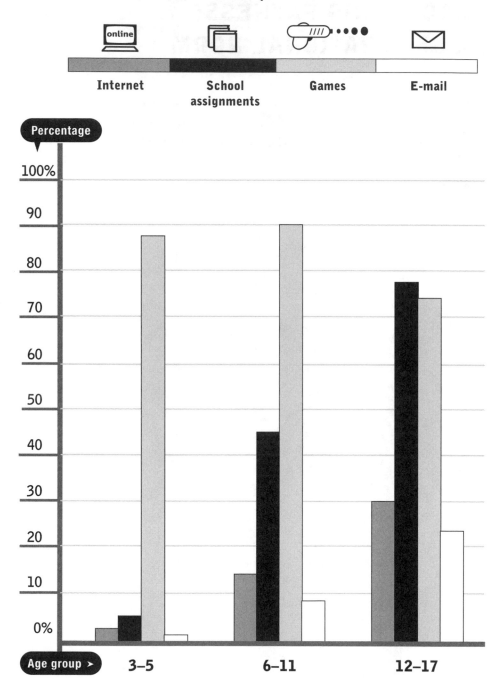

Generation Y

While the phrase "Generation X" quickly became a token of cultural—not to mention marketing—currency in the early 1990s, epitomized by such period films as *Reality Bites*, Generation Y has seen all the press of a sequel. Indeed, Generation Y (born between 1976 and 1985) has shaken off many attempts to be labeled. After resisting the mid-1990s belief that Yers—the first generation to be brought up around personal computers—were a coming "Net generation" that would soon dominate the U.S. economy with their high technical skills, Gen Y shrugged off the all-out labeling assault by PepsiCo's "Generation Next!" soda sales campaign. If Gen X was incomprehensible to marketers, Gen Y is overtargeted, and at least dimly proud of it. Cosmopolitan, media-savvy, and distant from traditional politics, these adolescents and young adults tend to identify first with the world as a whole, then with their close friends (or musical "scene"), and only after, with their county or city.

But demographers report that Gen Yers have succeeded at "marketing themselves." The group that graduated from college in 2000 had higher annual incomes in their first year in the labor force than any other class in U.S. history. Although high incomes might seem cause for excessive optimism or a hint of an impending economic conservatism, Generation Y maintains a reserved, yet well-defined and particularist, social awareness. Although Boomers participate in activist organizations more than they do, Gen Yers are more likely to express support for global causes, especially international peace and labor organization, as well as domestic social concerns. Indeed, Gen Yers by far have the highest rates of acceptance of gayness (they are less than half as likely as Boomers to say they would not like to have a gay neighbor). And most Gen Yers underestimate their worth; a substantial majority of those currently in college believe they will have a difficult time locating a job after graduation or will not be able to find one at all.

Yet however strong their short-term employment prospects may seem, America's demography threatens Generation Y's long-term economic fortunes. Some have predicted that Y's career advancement will be stifled; late Baby Boomers took corporate executive and governmental leadership positions in the early 1990s while still young and look likely to dominate these ranks for several more decades.

2

SEXES

Gender and Sexuality

Expectations of gender behavior—the role of being a
man or a woman—influence what people earn and how they spend it,
what they learn and how they are taught, who they vote for and who
votes for them, and certainly, how and whom they love. Gender at times
may seem one of life's basic differences, a constant fact of life. Popular
reference to "battles of the sexes" certainly implies that the teams (and
terms) are at least clearly delineated. But changing expectations for men
and women in America demonstrate that what we might be tempted to
believe are immutable characteristics given to each sex are, in fact,
shaped largely by the society that one lives in. The pressure to conform
to a "standard" gender role is being resisted by political movements—
feminist, gay, transgender—and by individuals living in defiance of the
identities society has attempted to assign them. Although the statistics
often do not keep pace with the ways in which people describe themselves, demographic research can reveal on which fronts the sexual revolution has most advanced.

Glass Ceilings, Sticky Floors, Pink Collars

2.1

Between 1950 and 2000, the percentage of working-age women in the labor force more than doubled, rising from 30 percent to 67 percent. This does not mean, of course, that in 1950 70 percent of women led leisurely lives. Instead, their work was often unpaid and undervalued. The same problem persists in the workforce. In 1961, a working woman earned fifty-nine cents to a man's dollar. Today, women average seventy-three cents to a man's dollar—the gap has closed only fourteen cents in forty years, and the pay disparity shows no sign of evening out in the near future.

A host of reasons can be offered to explain this disparity. Most obviously, simple sexism can prevent women from earning as much as comparable men, even though both the Equal Pay Act of 1963 and Title VII of the Civil Rights Act of 1964 prohibit unequal pay for "substantially equal" work performed by men and women. Enforcement of these laws, however, remains scattered, and it is exceedingly difficult to prove wage discrimination in court. As women entered the labor force in large numbers, pink-collar jobs emerged. These occupations held primarily by women usually provide far lower wages than jobs staffed predominantly by men. Firms whose employees are 76 to 90 percent male pay wages 40 percent higher than similar firms employing mostly women.

Women are also often blocked from advancing their careers to higher-earning positions. Working women are trapped not only by the Glass Ceiling, an invisible barrier that prevents them from rising to the upper echelons of corporate authority at nearly the rate of similarly qualified men, but in some occupations they are prevented from advancing at all in position or earning power—held back by a Sticky Floor.

MEDIAN INCOME BY SEX

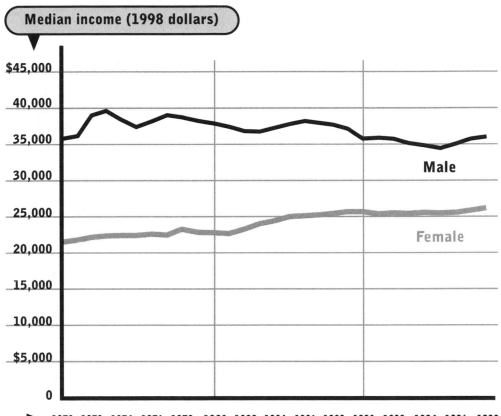

Median income (1998 dollars)

$45,000
40,000
35,000
30,000
25,000
20,000
15,000
10,000
$5,000
0

Male

Female

▶ 1970 1972 1974 1976 1978 1980 1982 1984 1986 1988 1990 1992 1994 1996 1998

Year

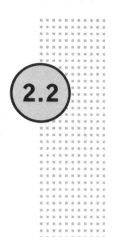

2.2

Sex × Race

Women of color are at a special disadvantage in the United States. Just as labor force participation and pay rates vary between genders, variation occurs between different races. Pay inequity is magnified. Some of this is because women of color are less likely to work in professional or managerial jobs than white men. A woman of color is subject to the issues that create wage disparities between races as well as those that create gaps between genders, and is especially prone to being stuck in undervalued jobs.

This double bind complicates study of pay discrepancy. Whereas the average woman earns 73 percent of what the average man earns, and the average Latino earns 61 percent of what the average white man earns, the average Latina (woman) earns only 50 percent of what the average white man earns. Moreover, in some instances, race "trumps" gender as a disadvantage to a worker. A white woman with a master's degree earns $42,002 annually, only $321 less than a black man with a master's, but a white man with a master's earns $17,854 more per year than a black man with a master's.

MEDIAN INCOME BY SEX AND RACE, 1998

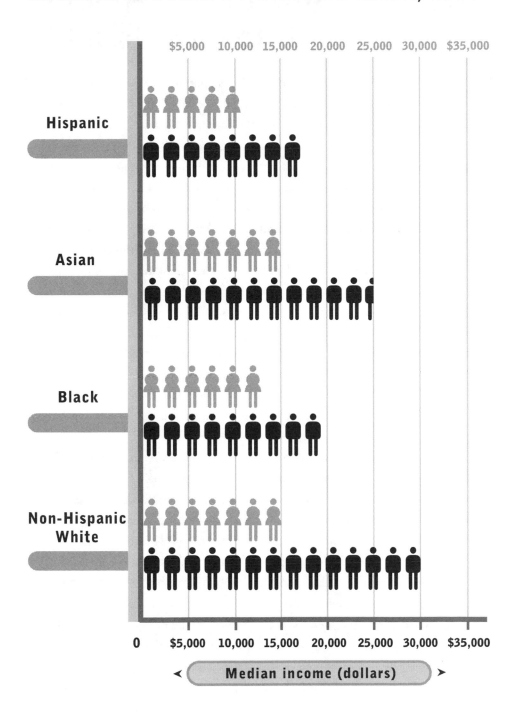

Out of the Home: Into the House?

As far as democratic ideals of representation and participation are concerned, it was one thing for Clinton devotees to dedicate 1996's presidential victory to "soccer moms" across the country, to actually elect a soccer-mom president would be something else altogether. Although "the women's vote" has become a commonplace—if questionably accurate—buzzword to encompass the varying political ideologies, social beliefs, and economic concerns of women in the United States, there remains a systemic underrepresentation of women of all kinds throughout American politics. The headlines that celebrated the victories of Jeanette Rankin (the first female representative, 1916), Shirley Chisholm (the first black female representative, 1968), or Tammy Baldwin (the first openly lesbian representative, 1998) only attest to the rarity with which women serve in Congress. In fact, 1992's celebrated Year of the Woman surge in elected female representatives succeeded only in moving the United States from fourth- to eleventh-lowest among twenty-five democratic nations in the proportion of women in legislatures. Only then did America approach the international average of 11 percent. (Although, of course, in 1992 women comprised not 11 percent but over 50 percent of the U.S. population.)

The difficulty is not with the voters, most of whom wish for a more equitable government and, all else equal, offer an edge to female candidates. But this does not mean that gender does not influence how things are equal, as voters are 18 percent more likely to vote for a woman campaigning on "women's issues" than one running on a platform that focuses on traditionally masculine issues like foreign policy or the economy. Moreover, the field of electable female candidates is narrowed by voters' expectations that not only must women running for office be exceptionally well qualified, but that they have already raised their children. Female candidates always risk media reprisal if they stray too far from stereotyped sex roles and interests. Although the major parties are beginning to realize that a female candidate is often an asset, before the 1990s it was a common practice for parties to run most of their female candidates in races that had already been deemed unwinnable.

The privilege of incumbency, though, remains the highest barrier to representation by women. A congress—or, for that matter, a county board—that started all male is bound to stay that way for a long time. For this reason, organizations like EMILY'S List offer money to female candidates to run in primaries, when an infusion of financial resources is most vital. Providing seed money to female candidates is one of very few ways that have been shown to accelerate the slow march to equal representation.

A WOMAN FOR PRESIDENT?

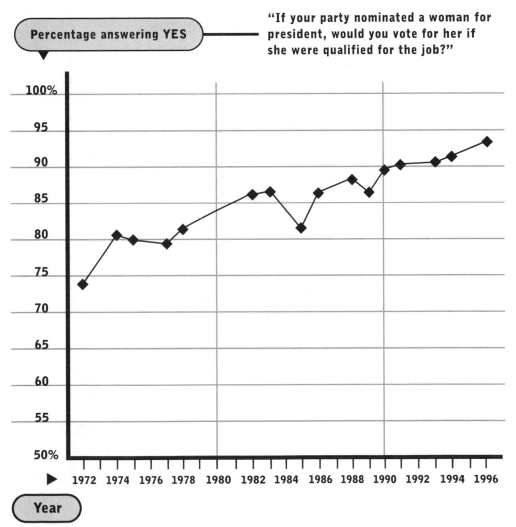

Percentage answering YES

"If your party nominated a woman for president, would you vote for her if she were qualified for the job?"

Year

THE ADVANCE OF WOMEN'S LIB

1841   Oberlin College becomes the first to grant undergraduate degrees to women.

1848   The Seneca Falls Convention drafts an agenda for the women's movement.

1878   A women's suffrage amendment is introduced into the U.S. Congress.

1916   Jeanette Rankin of Montana is elected to the U.S. House of Representatives.

1918   In New York v. Sanger, doctors win the right to give married patients birth-control information.

1920   The Nineteenth Amendment (identical to that introduced forty-two years earlier) is finally adopted.

1933   Frances Perkins is appointed secretary of labor.

1963   Congress prohibits sex discrimination in pay.

1964   Congress prohibits employment discrimination based on gender.

1966   The National Organization of Women (NOW) is formed.

1973   In Roe v. Wade, the Supreme Court legalizes abortion.

1986   Sexual harassment in the workplace is ruled illegal.

Women in Time

From the beginnings of feminism in America, concepts of "feminism" have expanded and have been hotly contested. Elizabeth Cady Stanton and Lucretia Mott organized the first Women's Rights Convention in Seneca Falls, New York, in 1848. After women won the hard-earned battle for suffrage in 1920, feminism dwindled, until World War II introduced "Rosie the Riveter" to the American labor force. Mass numbers of women entered the workforce, many only to be replaced at the war's end. The postwar climate pushed conservatism, normalcy, and pressure to be the perfect wife and mother, until Betty Friedan's *The Feminine Mystique* challenged suburban feminine malaise in 1963. Suddenly, the "second wave" of feminism began to move. The next fifteen years saw the founding of feminist liberation groups, the National Organization of Women (NOW), prohibition of sex discrimination in employment through Title VII of the Civil Rights Act, the elections of Shirley Chisholm and Bella Abzug to Congress, and the inauguration of *Ms.* magazine. It also witnessed the formation of groups like the National Black Feminist Organization and Radicalesbians by women who were frustrated by the reticence of mainstream, mostly white and heterosexual, feminist leaders to support or emphasize certain issues. In 1982, the Equal Rights Amendment, originally proposed in 1923 and predicted by many in the 1970s to be easily ratified, was defeated, signaling to many that the feminist movement was no longer needed or successful. The Reagan years saw a backlash against feminism from "angry white male" voters and attacks upon abortion rights, "unwed welfare mothers," and later, "feminazis."

In the 1990s, feminism became much more diffuse, concerned with issues of pay equity, sexual harassment, rape, pornography, and the status of women around the world. While the fading of a rhetoric of liberation signals the achievement of some goals, gender oppression continues, and today's tempered tone is due to the movement's institutionalization, not its dissolution. Many who do not call themselves "feminists" might do so if they did not take for granted a society no longer dominated by sexist or patriarchal ideas.

2.5

Feminist Values and the Fear of "Feminism"

Feminism is best understood as a set of concepts about the way gender roles should be performed in society. As with most terms that describe broad sets of belief, feminism includes contradictory ideas. While some strains of feminism advocate the open expression of female sexuality, for example, others concentrate on ending exploitive overemphasis on female appearance. Not surprisingly, the camps sometimes clash. Although all feminisms agree in their opposition to sexism, the sexism of a specific act is often debated. And at times, "feminism" appears to be a cultural term in danger of succumbing to its vagueness—much as "liberal" and "conservative" sometimes seem today—hosting too many viewpoints under its umbrella to name a single cohesive ideology. But unlike being "conservative" or "liberal," pronouncing oneself a supporter of feminism implies a personal commitment to changing the status quo. Or, as the National Organization of Women argues, to simply say "I am a feminist" can itself be empowering.

American attitudes toward feminism are mixed. Studies have shown that over 75 percent of women refuse to call themselves feminist even though a sizeable majority think that the women's movement has improved the lives of women, as well as men, full-time homemakers, and children. Why, then, the hesitancy to support feminism in name, despite the emphatic support of issues feminists have advocated?

Feminism today has both an image problem and an issues problem. Attacks from conservative pundits have successfully reestablished the 1970s image of the man-hating feminist in the popular mind. And feminism in the 1990s became increasingly concerned with the divisive and ultimately alienating topics of sex—from sexual harassment to pornography to the sexual liberation of women. Still, although young women and those who came of age during the second wave of feminism are more likely to support explicitly feminist goals, a majority of people in every generation support the pursuit of careers by married women, abortion rights, pay equity, and the ideals of gender equality—all important components of what has defined "feminism."

FEMINIST BENEFITS AND IDENTITIES BY GENERATION, 1996

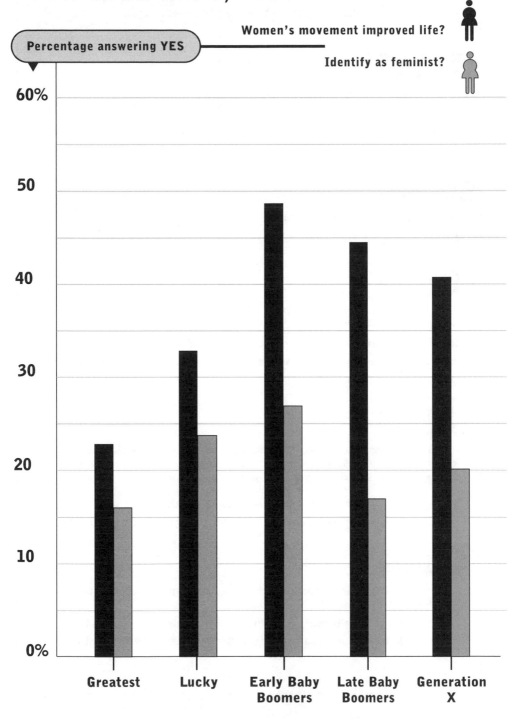

Percentage answering YES

Women's movement improved life?

Identify as feminist?

60%

50

40

30

20

10

0%

Greatest   Lucky   Early Baby Boomers   Late Baby Boomers   Generation X

THE COUNTERS AND THEIR COUNTS

Studies trying to ascertain the prevalence of gays have come up with wildly varying results. In some cases this is due to differences in method; in others, it is due to differences in focus.

1948 / 53

A. Kinsey et al., *Sexual Behavior in the Human Male*, and *Sexual Behavior in the Human Female*.

Males 37% had experienced homosexual orgasm; 4% exclusively homosexual.

Females 13% had experienced homosexual orgasm; 1–3% exclusively homosexual.

1974

M. Hunt, *Sexual Behavior in the 1970s*.

Males 25% had experienced orgasm through homosexual contact.

1993

J. Billy, K. Fanfer, W. Grady, and D. Klepingerm. "The Sexual Behavior of Men in the United States." *Family Planning Perspectives* 25 no. 2.

Of twenty- to thirty-nine-year-old noninstitutionalized males, 2% of sexually active men had had homosexual activity within the past ten years; 1% had been exclusively homosexual over that period.

1995

R. L. Sell, J. A. Wells, and D. Wypji. "The Prevalence of Homosexual Behavior and Attraction in the United States, the United Kingdom, and France: Results of National Population-Based Samples." *Archives of Sexual Behavior* 24 no. 3.

Males 20.8% reported homosexual behavior or attraction since age fifteen.

Females 17.8% reported homosexual behavior or attraction since age fifteen.

1998

T. Smith, *American Sexual Behavior: Trends, Socio-Demographic Differences, and Risk Behavior* (using General Social Survey data).

In 1998, 3.3% of sexually active men and 2.3% of sexually active women had had sex with someone of the same gender within the previous twelve months.

Counting in the Closet: Does It Matter How Many Americans Are Gay?

Gay, lesbian, bisexual, and transgender Americans face perhaps the harshest discrimination of any class of Americans today. Until quite recently, homosexuality was a taboo subject, mentioned only in whispered allusions and locker-room jeers. In fact, barely a century has passed since "homosexuality" was coined by doctors to describe individuals with loving or sexual attractions to members of the same sex. "Gay" only entered the popular American vocabulary about thirty years ago. While it was never controversial that about half the U.S. population was female, gay Americans are never enumerable by appearance alone and often unwilling to identify themselves.

The 1948 Kinsey Report, probably the most oft-repeated survey, estimated that one in ten Americans are gay or lesbian. Gay America, however, is resistant to accurate statistical counts, as many gay men and lesbians, for fear of reprisal by society, are leery to identify themselves to an anonymous survey taker. Different survey methods garner wildly different results, depending upon the vocabulary used and the composition of the survey group. Many Americans have had limited relationships with someone of the same sex but do not identify themselves as gay or lesbian. Many others find sexual orientation to be a fluid undetermined matter and freely shift their social identifications. The confusions around differences in how people identify their sexuality have led some to argue that statistical totals are irrelevant to many of the issues that gay Americans confront. Although this attitude has its kernel of truth, greater acceptance may depend on the recognition that gays and lesbians are already living throughout American neighborhoods and participating en masse in American politics, business, and culture.

Lavender Ghettos and the Rights Closet

Many myths about gayness still carry weight, in some parts of the country more than others. As a result, gays and lesbians have increasingly flocked to more tolerant areas. For example, estimates based on the 1990 census conclude that gays and lesbians reside in gay magnet cities New York, Los Angeles, and San Francisco at a rate double that of the population at large. Disproportionate concentration in urban centers—New York City's Chelsea and Washington's Dupont Circle, for example—and college towns—Ann Arbor, Michigan, and Madison, Wisconsin—has created oases where a variety of sexualities flourish, but has correspondingly depopulated other areas, where myths about homosexuality therefore go largely unchallenged.

Lavender ghettos—small urban pockets that serve as cultural refuges for the gay population—may eventually be unnecessary. A number of signs point

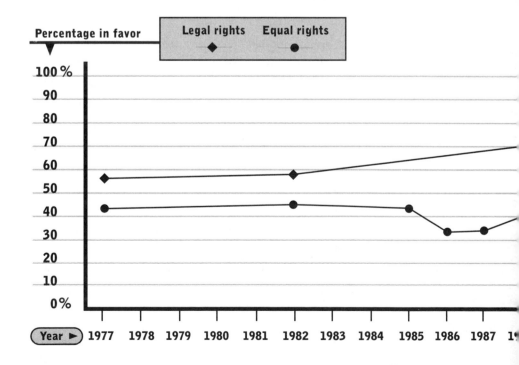

to increased acceptance of gayness by the U.S. population. Gallup reports that an increasing majority, from 56 percent in the late 1970s to 84 percent in 2000, believe that homosexuals should have equal rights in the job market. However, Americans' increasing willingness to argue in favor of equal rights for gays and lesbians is complemented by a reluctance to accept legal rights for same-sex relationships. In 1997, for example, the majority still supported the criminalization of same-sex relations. Gay Americans often come out only to find themselves in a "rights closet"—a society which believes gays and lesbians are to be protected and tolerated only as long as they remain invisible. This logic culminated in the 1993 creation of the U.S. military's "Don't ask, don't tell" policy, under which gay men and lesbians could serve in the military only as long as they kept their sexual preferences secret.

ATTITUDES TOWARD GAY RIGHTS

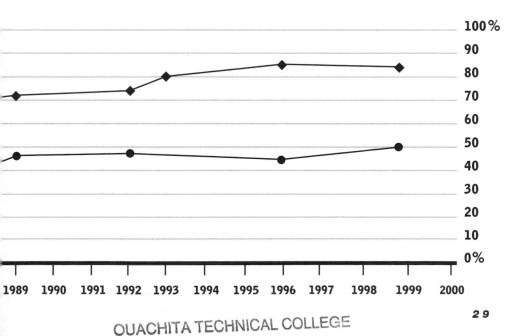

STATISTICS, RIOTS, AND RIGHTS

1948 The Kinsey Report's statistics on same-sex activity challenge the notion that straight is normal.

1951 An early movement organization, the Mattachine Society, is founded in Los Angeles.

1961 Illinois becomes the first state to repeal its sodomy laws.

1969 Police harassment at a New York bar sparks three days of rioting, signaling a new militancy.

1970 The first lesbian and gay–pride march takes place, in New York.

1985 President Reagan mentions AIDS for the first time—four years after the epidemic begins.

1992 President Clinton makes "Don't ask, don't tell" the rule for gays in the military.

2000 Vermont enacts "civil unions" law, allowing gays and lesbians most of the rights of straight couples.

From Mattachine to Stonewall to Queer

2.8

To be "queer" would seem to be a matter that involves only the most personal sexual behavior. But queer Americans face a host of issues unique to their social position. Gayness is one of the few traits that it is still socially acceptable—and in some subcultures, it seems, compulsory—to mock and deride. As recently as the 1980s, a "homosexual panic" defense was accepted by the courts to justify the murder of a gay man. Systemic discrimination against gay Americans remains commonplace, even though institutionalized homophobia has waned, as illustrated by the courts' rejection of the homosexual panic defense during the 1999 trial of Jonathan Schmitz for the murder of Scott Amedure after their appearance on the *Jenny Jones* show. Hate crimes, workplace discrimination, alienation from one's family and friends, lack of health benefits to one's partner, and prohibitions on same-sex relations in some states all perpetuate homosexuality's stigma.

Gay and lesbian activism occurs on a variety of fronts, from the courts to the legislatures, from the arts to the streets. After the founding of the Society for Human Rights in 1924, gay and lesbian rights organizations grew slowly, but the 1969 Stonewall riots in New York City jump-started the modern gay and lesbian movement. Today, there are at least twenty-five hundred lesbian and gay political, religious, student, or cultural organizations in the United States. Like any movement, it is diversified. Some groups stress nonconformity, while others seek assimilation into mainstream America. In the 1980s, the AIDS crisis forced mobilization of the gay population, and organizations like ACT UP successfully won attention and money for AIDS research from the silent Reagan government. Since the heydey of AIDS activism, gay male culture has tended to dominate queer politics, often to the exclusion of the lesbian community.

PEOPLES

Race, Ethnicity, and Identity

Identities of race and ethnicity carry with them different privileges, dangers, and expectations. In the American experience, these distinctions have been most evident between blacks and whites. But a monochrome view of race obscures the shifting mosaic of ethnic and racial identities. The era of majority/minority Is fast fading—whites and blacks are becoming two minorities alongside others. This complexity was reflected in the 2000 census, which found that 6.8 million Americans identify with more than one race. Furthermore, the racial categories we use are being hotly contested. After all, the picture of race in America is more complex than even an exhaustive enumeration of ethnic groups could portray. People are not born in the little boxes—white, black, Asian, Hispanic—found on the survey forms of bureaucrats and social scientists. The box one chooses (or refuses) is decided both by the identity society imposes and by the identity one adopts, for reasons political and personal, assembled from fragments of the past and present.

3.1

African Americans: Race, Racism, and the Census

Unlike immigrants from Europe, Africans generally came to America in bondage and were torn from family, language, and tribe. While preserving what tradition they could, their identities were indelibly marked by the actions and decisions of whites. In the Civil War and in the struggle culminating in the 1960s, African Americans broke through these barriers and began to redefine the American conception of race always an uneasy relationship between imposed identities and official racial categories.

Official categories have sometimes reflected a perverse worldview. The 1890 census, for instance, tried to classify those with African ancestry as "black," "mulatto," "quadroon," or "octoroon," depending on how much "black blood" they had. The 1870 census warned respondents that "important scientific results" depended on accurately distinguishing between "blacks" and "mulattos." At various times in the nineteenth century, white Americans mined the census data to show that emancipation led to insanity for black people, to prove that blacks were "demographically inferior" and doomed to extinction, and to measure the cash value of the slave population.

This sordid history of classifying people by race has tempted many to make statistics, social science, and the government "color blind." But the legacy of discrimination in the social, political, and economic systems cannot be changed without accounting for—and counting—race. After the Civil War, Washington attempted to use census data to enforce black voting rights. And census data have been used—much more effectively—since the Voting Rights Act of 1965, to enforce voting rights, affirmative action, and school integration. The importance of data on race was emphasized when, under the Reagan administration, several government agencies stopped classifying their beneficiaries by race in their records. Without such classification it was difficult to discern whether the agencies' programs were discriminating against people of color. The government did succeed in becoming color blind, but only by blinding itself to discrimination.

INTERROGATING RACE

The Emancipation Proclamation did not end the obsession with racial classification, and what the census taker demanded has varied quite a lot through the years.

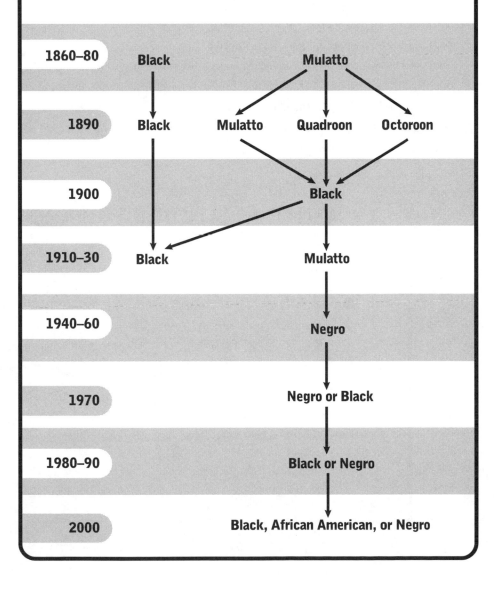

1860–80	Black — Mulatto
1890	Black — Mulatto — Quadroon — Octoroon
1900	Black
1910–30	Black — Mulatto
1940–60	Negro
1970	Negro or Black
1980–90	Black or Negro
2000	Black, African American, or Negro

A Revolution in White Attitudes

Just half a century ago, the way white people felt about black people was profoundly different than today. As white people constituted the vast majority of the population, their actions and attitudes were enormous obstacles to freedom and equality in America.

In the 1940s, most whites opposed blacks and whites attending the same schools, and most thought that whites should be given preference in hiring decisions. And if mixing in the classroom or the workplace was suspect, mixing in marriage was beyond the pale—in 1958, only 4 percent of whites approved of whites and blacks marrying each other.

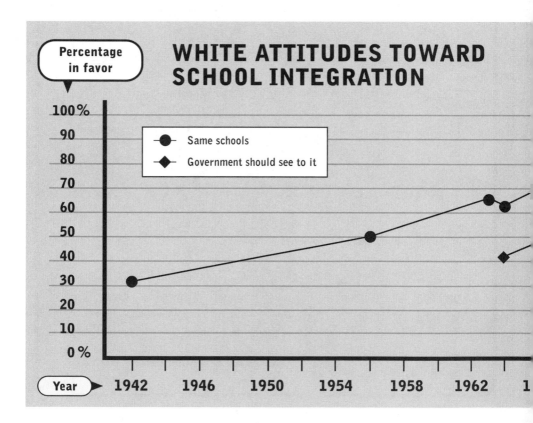

But during the intervening years, these attitudes were transformed by the activism of blacks, judicial decisions, legislative acts, and greater interaction between the races. The last is particularly significant, as the transformation of white attitudes has been less a matter of old people changing their minds, than of those old people being replaced by young people who came of age in a different world.

Now, hardly any whites profess opposition to integrated schools or endorse the preferential hiring of white people. Contemporary white attitudes are more ambivalent, however, than these statistics convey. Views on integrated schools are a case in point. While support for integration has become nearly universal, support for government intervention to make such integration a reality has declined from 47 percent in 1970 to less than 30 percent today. And, while few white parents object to their children going to school with a few black children, only about 80 percent would be content with a school that was half black and only about 40 percent with one that was mostly black.

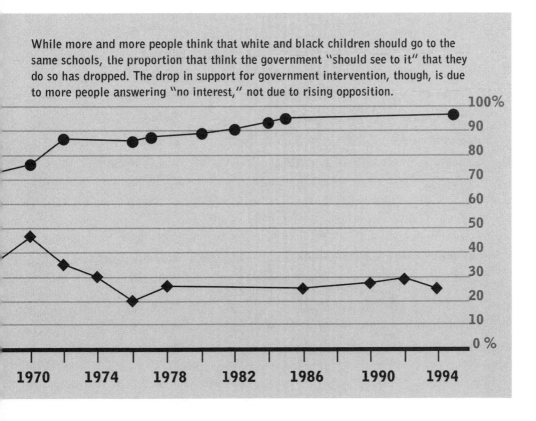

While more and more people think that white and black children should go to the same schools, the proportion that think the government "should see to it" that they do so has dropped. The drop in support for government intervention, though, is due to more people answering "no interest," not due to rising opposition.

WHITE ETHNICS

White people are not all the same. When asked their "ancestry," they identify with a multitude of nationalities, ethnicities, and localities.

Abruzzese	Finnish	Ossetian
Albanian	Frisian	Pennsylvania German
Alsatian	Greek Cypriote	Piedmontese
Andalusian	Hamburger	Polish
Andorran	Husel	Pomeranian
Basilicatan	Irish	Pugliese
Basque	Italian	Romansch
Bavarian	Karelian	Ruthenian
Belgian	Kashubian	Saxon
Belourussian	Ladinian	Swiss
Berliner	Lapp	Scotch Irish
Bioko	Lemko	Silesian
British	Liechtensteiner	Spaniard
Calabrian	Livonian	Sudetenlander
Campanian	Lombardian	Ticinese
Channel Islander	Lorrainian	Tirolean
Cornish	Lubecker	Transylvanian
Corsican	Luxemburger	Trentino
Cycladic Islander	Macedonian	Triestian
Cypriot	Madeiran	Valle d'Aosta
Czech	Manx	Voytak
Danish	Monegasque	Wallachian
Dutch	Northern Irish	Walloon
East German	Norwegian	Windish
Faeroe Islander	Occitan	Yugoslavian

White People: Molding and Melting Nationalities

Today, the descendants of European immigrants to the United States, 69 percent of Americans, tend to identify themselves as "white." Their ancestors' nationalities and ethnic identities rarely appear relevant to their public lives. White ethnicity is often only a private matter, reserved for the rituals of family—weddings, funerals, holidays, reunions. For public, social purposes, such colorings have melted into simple "white." But the story of how whiteness came to envelop so many in its cloak of racial privilege is not a simple one.

For starters, the ethnic identities white Americans now lay claim to—German, Italian, Irish, and so on—often differ from those that their immigrant ancestors held. To understand this, it is necessary to recall the political contours of the continent from which they came: Italy was not a state until 1861, Germany formed only in 1871, and the Austro-Hungarian empire continued to subsume Czechs, Magyars, Croats, and others until the end of the First World War. Prior to the formation of modern nation-states—and often only afterward—it was regional and local ties that defined individuals.

For many, becoming a nationality happened in the United States, not in Europe. For instance, it took decades after disembarking for Romans, Sicilians, Neapolitans, and Calabrians to become "Italians." The creation of a national identity was not an inevitability, but instead the result of organizing people and creating institutions, whether social clubs or political machines, to gain strength from numbers in the face of a prejudiced U.S. society. Indeed, such strength was part of what made assimilation as equals possible.

Native Americans: Demography and Decisions

The Native American population registered tremendous growth throughout the twentieth century. In 1900, the census counted 237,196 Native Americans; in 2000, the figure was 2,475,956 Native Americans. Much of this gain is the result of recovery from the demographic devastation suffered in the centuries following the arrival of Europeans. But it also reflects a renewed resistance to assimilation.

From 1950 to 1960, the census records a 46.5 percent leap in Native American population. Certainly, growth this rapid could not be caused by a wave of newborns alone. Much of the rise was the result of reform in census enumeration procedures: 1960 was the first year in which respondents selected their own race rather than having it decided for them by a census taker. Apparently, the 1950 census had failed to count as Native American many who lived outside reservations as well as many who identified as Native American, yet did not "look like an Indian."

The following censuses recorded similarly high rates of growth. Between 1970 and 1980, for example, the increase was 72.4 percent (versus 11.4 percent for the U.S. population as a whole). Demographers have estimated that more than 60 percent of this growth can be attributed to a rise in the willingness of Americans to identify with their Native American ancestry. These shifts in identity may have been stimulated by the Native American activism of the 1960s and 1970s—which included occupations of Alcatraz Island, Wounded Knee, and the Bureau of Indian Affairs in Washington, D.C.—as well as the growing sense of a broader Native American ethnic identity that did not require affiliation with any particular tribe.

As of 1980, less than 20 percent of Americans with some Native American ancestry considered their race to be "American Indian." Thus, the future of the Native American population will continue to depend not only on the demographics of fertility and mortality, but also on changing self-perceptions and an evolving ethnic consciousness.

NATIVE AMERICAN POPULATION COUNTS

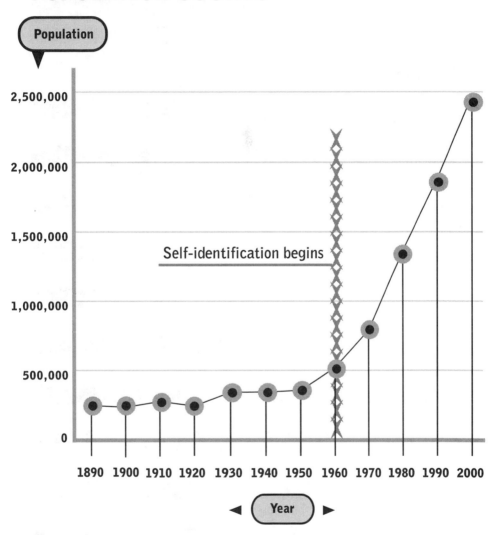

SELF-IDENTIFIED RACE OF SELECTED U.S. HISPANICS, 1990

The census requests respondents to specify their race, their ancestry, and whether they are "Hispanic." Often, "Hispanic" is seen as a racial category in its own right, but the data resist so straightforward an interpretation.

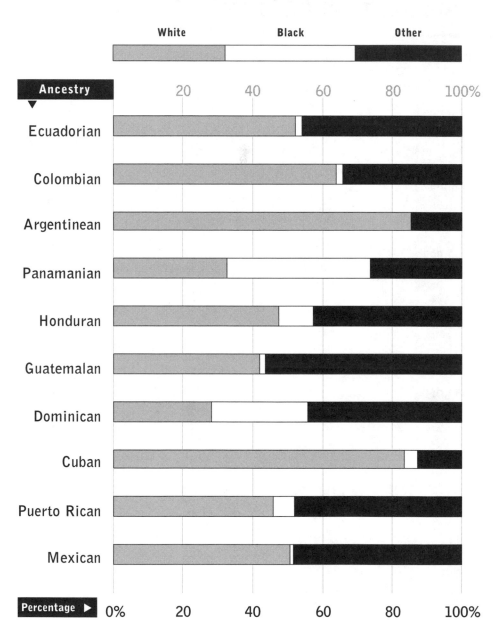

What Is "Hispanic"?

While the Southwest has had a large Spanish-speaking population since the sixteenth century, long before the area became U.S. territory, Latinos have become major players in American cities only since the 1965 liberalization of immigration law. Now they are quickly redefining America and the ways in which America views itself.

Those with roots in Latin America fit awkwardly into the U.S. racial system. Insofar as they share an identity, it is one founded on language, not complexion, which ranges from deepest black to starkest white. The nations of Latin America themselves have conceptions of race quite different from those of the United States. In the Dominican Republic, for instance, one is "white" if one has any European ancestry at all. In the United States, on the other hand, one "black" parent leads most to consider a person "black" or, in the past, "mulatto." Needless to say, Dominican immigrants can find the American mode of racism rather confusing.

The census asks separate questions on race and on Hispanic identification. When Hispanics come to the race question, they often fail to see where they might fit into the U.S. racial system. It was not until 1980—at the behest of Hispanic leaders seeking civil-rights protection for their community—that the census began to explicitly count "Hispanics." But whether identities founded on language, nationality, or color will gain primacy among America's burgeoning population of "Latinos" remains contested and problematic.

3.6

Asian American Diversity

Asian Americans have had a rather uneven experience in the United States. The Chinese and Japanese were singularly excluded from immigration in the late nineteenth and early twentieth centuries, and Japanese Americans were deemed so suspect in their loyalty as to be interned during the Second World War (with the help, it might be noted, of census data). During the trade deficit worries of the 1980s, Japan-bashing was implicitly condoned by the government. Today, on the other hand, Asian Americans tend to be stereotyped as hard-working, highly educated, and affluent. This combination of respect and resentment has made it difficult to combat what remains a confining, if ambivalent, stereotype. Globalization has led to the permeation (or cooption) of traditionally Asian motifs and genres into American popular culture, with varying degrees of authenticity. This is seen by some Asian Americans as a possibility that older stereotypes will break down and by others as only more evidence that, no matter how Americanized, concepts of Asian origin still carry with them ideas of the exotic and foreign.

The "Asian American" experience, though, varies greatly between nationalities and the circumstances in which their immigrant generations departed. The experiences of Americans from China, Korea, India, the Philippines, Japan, Vietnam, Laos, and Cambodia often share little economically, linguistically, or culturally. There is great diversity among Americans whose descendants came from China 150 years ago, Korean children adopted internationally in the 1970s and 1980s, and a family of immigrants from India today. The statistics say that a high proportion of Korean Americans are self-employed—45 percent of those working in Los Angeles, for instance. Such pursuits are possible because Korean immigrants bring an average of over $18,000 with them to the United States. Asian Americans who have come from Vietnam, Laos, and Cambodia have seldom been so lucky. As refugees fleeing the Vietnam War's aftermath, such immigrants have tended to be impoverished and poorly educated. In addition, government policy ensured that these populations were dispersed throughout the United States, preventing enclaves of mutual support from developing. The 1990 census documents the anomaly that Chinese Americans have a higher poverty rate than all Americans as well as a higher median family income. This is largely because of the wide gulf between different Chinese Americans. "Downtown Chinese" are mostly rural Chinese and immigrants from Taiwan and Hong Kong, who cluster in Chinatowns with varying degrees of mobility, whereas "uptown Chinese" are comprised mostly of American-born Chinese and well educated, professional immigrants who arrived under student or skilled-labor visas.

EDUCATIONAL ATTAINMENT OF SELECTED ASIAN NATIONALITIES, 1990

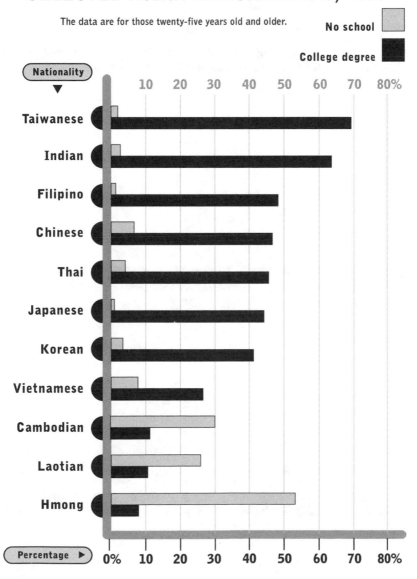

The data are for those twenty-five years old and older.

No school

College degree

POPULATION STRUCTURES, 2000

Each horizontal bar represents the population of the designated
age and sex of a particular group. The more pyramidal the structure,
the greater the potential for growth.

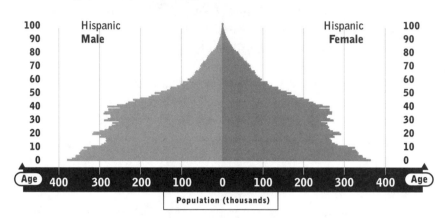

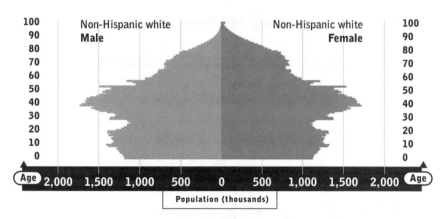

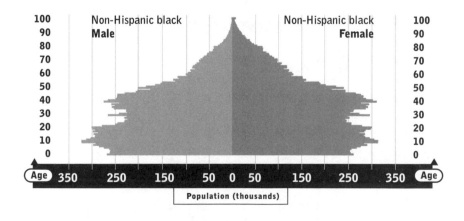

America's Developing Diversity

The demographic roots of America's diversity lie in its deep history of immigration. But the development of this diversity is shaped by more subtle factors: fertility, mortality, and the relative ages and compositions of different ethnic groups.

The white population is aging and stabilizing in size, whereas the Latino population is young and growing rapidly. Given these trends, it is projected that by 2060, non-Hispanic whites will be a minority, constituting slightly less than 50 percent of the population. Latinos will constitute 27 percent, African Americans 13 percent, and Asian Americans 9.8 percent.

How we will interpret these changes, though, is far less predictable than the changes themselves. In the past, such projections have provided the grounds for ideologies of racial competition. But as whites lose their demographic dominance, their ability to set the terms of America's discussion of race will presumably decline as well, widening the space for people of color to redefine the way Americans think about race. It is quite possible that by 2060 our projections will appear, though perhaps not inaccurate, anachronistic.

IMMIGRANTS

Crossing Borders

That America is a nation of immigrants is a commonplace notion; it is less noted that this makes it uniquely fit for a world in which transnational flows of goods, capital, ideas, art—as well as people—are of mounting importance. But when America has been given the world's tired and poor, its gut reaction has often been to send them back. Responses to immigration tend to reflect racist, economic, and political reasons—a combination at once explosive and difficult to untangle. Washington's regulation of immigration from Mexico, for example, has been largely a product of conflict between employers seeking cheap labor and workers seeking high wages, but economic concerns slide readily into racism as individuals try to justify exclusion or exploitation. Likewise, while Cold War geopolitics welcomed Vietnamese, Russians, Cubans, and others from communist countries with open arms, this political response did not preclude economic consequences or racial incidents. The economic prosperity of the 1990s, though, led to an unusually broad base of support for liberal immigration policies. However, long-lasting tolerance will require both a global perspective and an equitable globalization.

The History of Immigration: "Close the Door Behind You"

4.1

American immigration politics are, at base, ironic. On the one hand, a nativist distrust of new immigrants is firmly established in American culture and laws; even the Constitution, written barely a decade after independence, requires the president to have been born on native soil. Yet America itself is quintessentially a country of immigrants, with very few of its population claiming wholly indigenous ancestry. A quick survey of the history of immigration evidences a cycle of assimilation and nativism, as second-, third- and later-generation Americans turn against the open borders that allowed their forebears to seek opportunity in the United States.

Historically, most immigrants have come across the Atlantic. The first waves of immigrants were from Northern Europe; settlers from the British Isles, Scandinavia, and the German provinces came, mingled, and began to build the United States. Following on their heels were Italians, Poles, Russians, Southern Slavs, Chinese, and Japanese. While those from Southern and Eastern Europe were not always kindly welcomed, the earlier immigrants most resented the Chinese, whose passages were blocked by the Chinese Exclusion Act of 1882. Eastern European immigration was similarly restricted—though not so completely—by the quota system imposed in 1921.

The economic hardships of the Great Depression and stringent admissions policies of the Second World War reduced the "huddled masses" to scattered handfuls. But subsequent peace and prosperity in the postwar decades ensured that more would want to come. Newcomers to the United States have been arriving in increasing numbers since the 1940s. And the 1965 repeal of the quota system allowed new waves of Latin Americans and Asians to enter the country, forever changing America's national complexion.

While the politics of immigration continue to be hotly contested, the 1990s saw further increases in immigrant numbers. During 1998, 660,447 legal immigrants, 44,829 refugees, and an estimated 275,000 illegal immigrants entered the United States.

A HISTORY OF IMMIGRATION

1882
Chinese Exclusion Act: the beginning of the suspension of Chinese immigration. First time United States restricts immigration based on race.

1921
Quota System is created, primarily to limit Eastern European migration. Immigration is capped at 3% of the 1910 population of the country of origin.

1986
Immigration Reform and Control Act provides amnesty for millions of illegal immigrants. It also provides for tougher measures to fight illegal immigration.

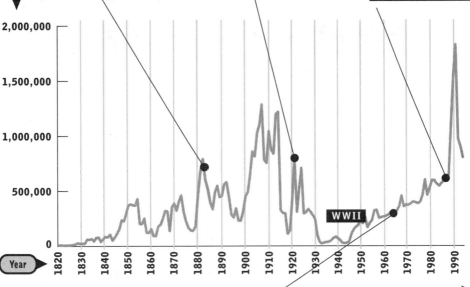

Number of immigrants

Year

WWII

2,000,000
1,500,000
1,000,000
500,000
0

1820 1830 1840 1850 1860 1870 1880 1890 1900 1910 1920 1930 1940 1950 1960 1970 1980 1990

1790
Naturalization begins. Free white persons who have lived in the United States for two years or longer are granted citizenship.

1965
The Quota System is eliminated. Each country is allowed the same number of immigrants per year (excluding countries from the Western hemisphere who have unlimited immigration privileges).

1996
Illegal Immigration Reform and Immigrant Responsibility Act is passed. Besides strengthening agencies that fight illegal immigration, this act also takes away public benefits rights from legal immigrants.

IMMIGRANTS ADMITTED INTO THE UNITED STATES BY CONTINENT, 1998

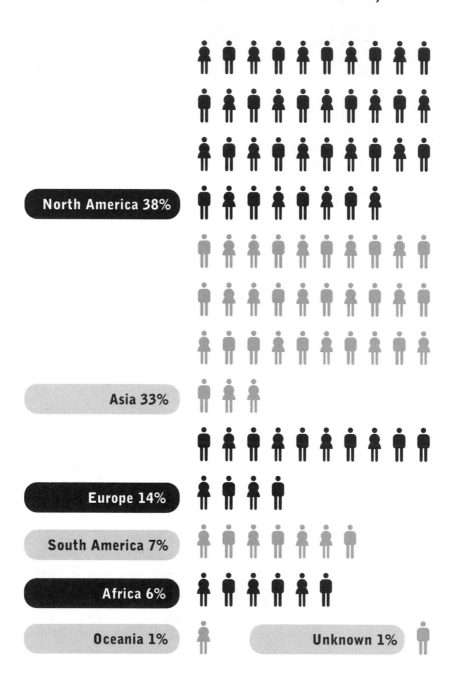

North America 38%

Asia 33%

Europe 14%

South America 7%

Africa 6%

Oceania 1%

Unknown 1%

Origins:
From North to South

By the late 1990s, immigrants from Latin America constituted a majority of the foreign-born population, and over a quarter of this population had immigrated from Asia. Now, less than one-fifth of the foreign-born population is European. The ethnic and national composition of the immigrant population today has shifted dramatically since 1960, when Europeans accounted for the bulk of first-generation immigrants.

Much of this shift in immigrant origins is accounted for by the 1965 liberalization of immigration law. However, liberal laws alone do not draw people to the United States. The two predominant countries of origin today—Mexico and the Philippines—have histories inextricably entangled with that of the States. The Philippines' legacy of colonization by the United States following the Spanish-American War and a continuing U.S. military presence after the Second World War have—perhaps ironically—created social and political conditions that make immigration to the States appear attractive and plausible.

Destinations: Gateway Cities and Immigrant Clusters

Immigrants and their descendants are responsible for populating the vast majority of the United States. However, upon arrival, new immigrants have not settled evenly across the country. Nineteenth- and early-twentieth-century immigrants, mostly from Europe, tended to settle in large gateway cities like New York, Chicago, or Boston (although immigrants from Scandinavia tended to settle in more rural parts of the country, like Minnesota and Wisconsin). Eventually, as these immigrants melted into the American pot, they dispersed more widely, first to gateway city suburbs and later across the rest of the United States.

Today's immigrants have also gathered mainly in a few ports of entry. During the 1990s, over 65 percent of all immigrants to the United States resided in just ten of the nation's almost three hundred metropolitan areas. The New York and Los Angeles metropolitan areas led the pack with well over a million immigrants each during the decade, followed by San Francisco, Miami, and Chicago. The last five of the top ten—Washington, Houston, Dallas, San Diego, Boston—together received less than either New York or Los Angeles alone.

Why do immigrants continue to come to these same gateway areas? The answer lies largely in U.S. immigration law's strong bias toward family reunification, which tends to occur in chains linking family members and friends to common destinations. There is also the need for immigrants from countries of similar backgrounds, languages, and cultures to live in communities where they will receive social and economic support. This is especially the case for less-skilled immigrants, who are more dependent on family and friends for assistance in gaining employment through the informal job networks that exist in metropolitan magnet areas.

But how long will it take newer immigrant groups, primarily from Latin America and Asia, to disperse to other parts of the country? There are signs that the diffusion is already happening in areas where low-skilled labor is in demand for service and blue-collar jobs like meatpacking and construction. Specialized technology jobs for which there is a dearth of sufficiently educated native-born workers are another force pulling immigrants into the heartland. Yet the bulk of the new and recent immigrant groups continue to cling to the handful of gateway magnets with the highest drawing power.

WHERE THE IMMIGRANTS LANDED, 1990–99

Each dot represents twenty-five thousand people.

Dots show each state's concentration, but the actual location of any given dot is arbitrary.

	IMMIGRANT MAGNET METROS — Number of immigrants, 1990–99	
1.	New York	1,408,543
2.	Los Angeles	1,257,925
3.	San Francisco	494,189
4.	Miami	420,488
5.	Chicago	363,662
6.	Washington	267,175
7.	Houston	214,262
8.	Dallas-Fort Worth	173,500
9.	San Diego	159,691
10.	Boston	137,634

A Land of Many Tongues: The Politics of Speaking

America's multitude of languages—ranging from Armenian to Hmong and from Korean to English—has proven one of the most contentious aspects of its immigrant nature. Linguistic diversity can be an asset in the global economy—for instance, Miami has become a key hub for U.S.–Latin American business. However, not being able to communicate with one's neighbor can be isolating, even enraging.

The Census Bureau has attempted to ascertain the extent of "linguistic isolation." A household is considered isolated if no occupants older than thirteen are able to speak English "very well." So defined, nearly 25 percent of Mexican Americans, 65 percent of Hmong Americans, and 36 percent of Chinese Americans are linguistically isolated. Of course, often language speakers cluster and may be far from isolated within their communities, but they do have difficulty participating in the U.S.'s national political, social, and economic life.

The problems have led to fierce debates over bilingual education and the possibility of making English the "official language." But whether linguistic diversity is a problem or an asset, immigrants and the children of immigrants continue to learn English as they have in the past. Some historical perspective may help: German Americans continued to publish German-language newspapers and take advantage of bilingual education well into the twentieth century. In 1940, more than half of rural, second-generation German immigrants spoke German as their first language.

LINGUISTIC ISOLATION BY GROUP, 1990

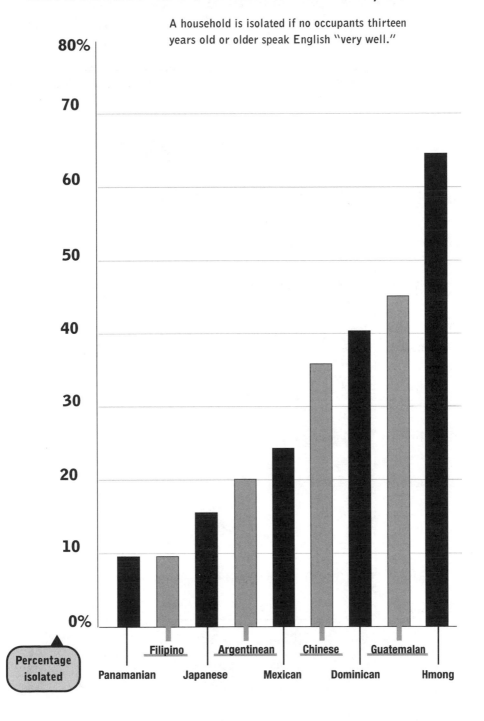

A household is isolated if no occupants thirteen years old or older speak English "very well."

Percentage isolated

Panamanian, Filipino, Japanese, Argentinean, Mexican, Chinese, Dominican, Guatemalan, Hmong

MEASURING THE DIASPORAS, 1997

Diasporas that constitute large proportions of their nation can have significant political and economic clout in their home country.

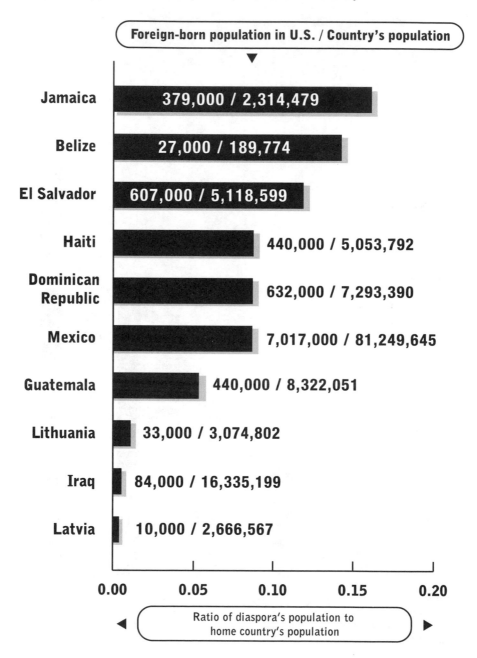

Foreign-born population in U.S. / Country's population

Jamaica	379,000 / 2,314,479
Belize	27,000 / 189,774
El Salvador	607,000 / 5,118,599
Haiti	440,000 / 5,053,792
Dominican Republic	632,000 / 7,293,390
Mexico	7,017,000 / 81,249,645
Guatemala	440,000 / 8,322,051
Lithuania	33,000 / 3,074,802
Iraq	84,000 / 16,335,199
Latvia	10,000 / 2,666,567

0.00   0.05   0.10   0.15   0.20

Ratio of diaspora's population to home country's population

Diaspora Politics

During the 1990s, it became clear that international movements of trade and capital were of crucial political importance. The role of movements of people has not always been as obvious. The political efficacy of immigrant diasporas rests both on their ability to influence events in their countries of origin and to influence U.S. foreign policy toward those countries.

Immigrants from Mexico and the Dominican Republic, for instance, have become important sources of campaign funding in their home countries. Moreover, the remittances they send home to family give them influence. For Mexico, these remittances constitute the third largest source of revenue. Recognizing their clout, Mexican candidates made campaign stops in U.S. cities during Mexico's 2000 presidential race. And on election day, immigrants sometimes choose to drive or fly back to vote. In Mexico's election, polling stations prepared for some seventy-five thousand voters were setup in towns along the U.S.-Mexican border.

Perhaps, though, the most dramatic example of a diaspora influencing its country of origin's politics was when an American citizen who had been a career bureaucrat in the U.S. government was elected president of Lithuania in 1998.

The Cuban and Taiwanese communities provide notable examples of diasporas affecting U.S. foreign policy. Through congressional lobbying, the Taiwanese have succeeded in obtaining military hardware and limited diplomatic recognition for their country. The Cuban diaspora has worked to maintain U.S. diplomatic and economic pressure on Havana. When five-year-old Elián González was brought to shore, attempts to return him to his father in Cuba led Miami's mayor, leading politicians, and the boy's extended family to all directly defy the federal government. The need for an armed invasion of the relatives' house to extricate the boy demonstrated the extent to which the Cuban diaspora has been willing to act as a political force independent of Washington.

Refugees and Asylum Seekers: Yearning to Breathe Free

Some come to the United States to advance their life dreams. Others come because their homelands are hellish. Washington classifies entrants fleeing their home countries into two categories: refugees and asylum seekers. Refugees are granted an American visa in their home country; asylum seekers flee their country first and hope to be granted a visa upon arrival.

The decision to grant or withhold refugee status is heavily political. It is an implied denigration of the conditions prevailing in the immigrant's country of origin and, depending on the U.S. government's role in that country, of American foreign policy as well.

After the United States withdrew from Vietnam, many Vietnamese, Cambodians, and Laotians were permitted to immigrate. Those leaving communist Cuba have received a similar welcome. On the other hand, the U.S. government was reluctant to accept Central Americans fleeing the civil wars, revolutions, and terrorism that engulfed those countries throughout the 1980s. This reluctance led to a "sanctuary movement" in which illegal Central American immigrants were hidden in churches throughout the United States.

Refugees and asylum seekers continue to arrive in the post–Cold War era. In fiscal year 1998, 83,000 refugees were admitted and 12,951 persons were granted asylum.

THE TRAUMA OF ESCAPE

When Indochinese immigrants in San Diego were surveyed in 1983,
it was found that the vast majority had feared for their lives while fleeing.
Many of those who made it had fended off attacks.

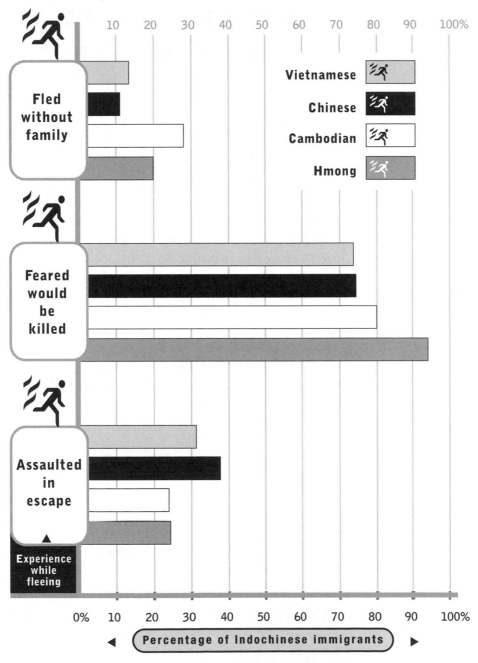

Fled without family

Vietnamese
Chinese
Cambodian
Hmong

Feared would be killed

Assaulted in escape

Experience while fleeing

Percentage of Indochinese immigrants

4.7

Illegal Immigration: American Fantasies of the South

The Immigration and Naturalization Service (INS) estimates that at least 5 million people reside in the United States illegally, and about 275,000 enter the United States illegally each year. The majority of these immigrants are from Mexico. Most come north to earn better lives for themselves or their families. According to one survey, 59 percent of men and 42.6 percent of women who have illegally immigrated from Mexico had economic motives.

The reactions of American citizens tend to spring from economic motives as well. While workers fear low-wage competition, employers often look forward to the resulting reduction in labor costs. U.S. immigration policies toward Mexicans reflect the interplay of these interests.

The racial classifications of the 1930 U.S. Census equated "Mexican" with "Mexican laborer." And during the Great Depression, about five hundred thousand Mexicans—many American citizens—were deported in an attempt to provide more jobs for established whites. During World War II, on the other hand, the United States suffered from labor shortages and began the Bracero program to bring Mexicans north to labor. After the Bracero program ended in 1964, Mexican immigration to the States continued—sometimes legally, sometimes illegally. Established Americans not only tend to think of Mexico as a developing land of factories—the *maquiladoras* that have spread across the border in the wake of NAFTA—but as itself a factory of 100 million. The Mexico Factory produces a single product for export north: the Laborer, a sometimes useful, but always socially dangerous tool to be employed in times of workforce need.

Even when the debates over the conditions for legality come to a close, those over enforcement continue. When the Immigration Reform and Control Act of 1986 passed, not only were some 2.7 million illegal immigrants—not necessarily Mexican—granted amnesty, but employers were chagrined to find that *they* could be fined for hiring undocumented workers. It is a rather different situation when the penalty instead is imposed on the worker, as the INS's recent "Operation Vanguard" made clear. INS deportations of scores of undocumented meatpacking workers served to make workforces frightened and deferent—employers welcomed the campaign; labor unions lambasted it.

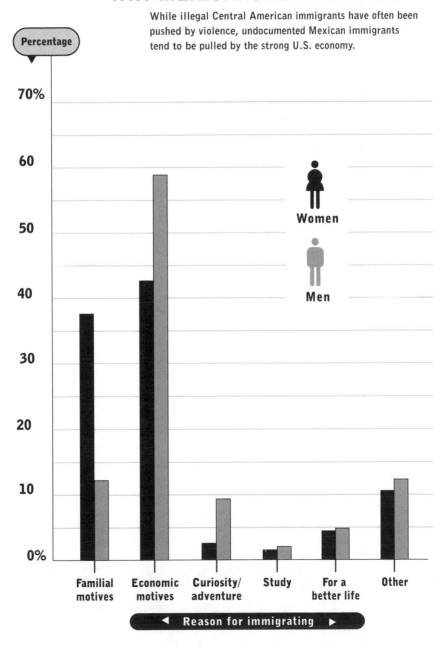

WHY MEXICANS MAKE THE MOVE

While illegal Central American immigrants have often been pushed by violence, undocumented Mexican immigrants tend to be pulled by the strong U.S. economy.

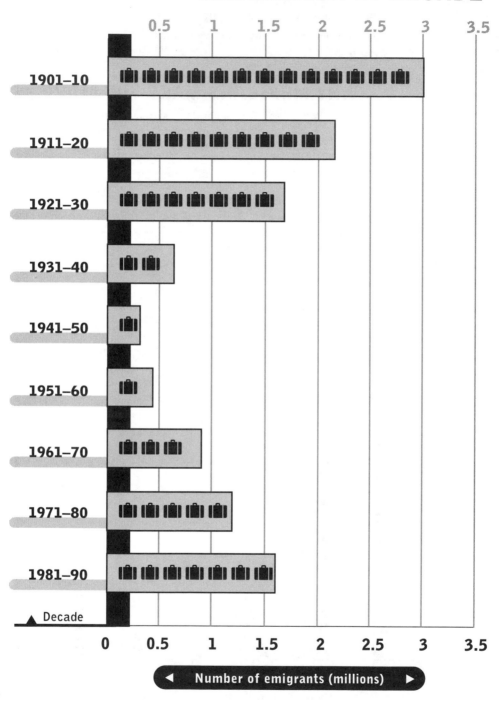

EMIGRATION BY DECADE

Number of emigrants (millions)

Emigration: Migrant Laborers and Belabored Emigrés

4.8

While new immigrants continue to surge through America's borders, a trickle flows out. Many of these are immigrants who came to earn money in the vast U.S. economy and are now returning home to family and friends. Other emigres are native-born Americans seeking escape from criminal laws or shelter from financial regulations. Still others hope to re-create their cultural life and personal identity by moving overseas.

The largest exodus was during the first decade of the twentieth century, when 3 million persons left the United States. The smallest occurred under the tight patriotism and tighter labor market of World War II–era America. Finding economic prosperity on the home front and few secure destinations overseas, only 281,000 emigrated.

Today, Mexico tops not only the immigration charts, but also the emigration charts. Many Latin American immigrants are seasonal migrant laborers who come to work for a few harvest months in the fields and orchards of the North to earn enough to subsist in their homelands for the rest of the year.

However, while the expansive bureaucratic net of the Immigration and Naturalization Service permits a detailed count of legal immigrants to the United States, emigration, lacking a clearly defined regulatory organ, is much more difficult to accurately measure. Although immigrants are not always welcome, neither is a nation proud to have its population flee. Indeed, the most recent well known wave of emigration from the States—the Vietnam-era flight of draft-eligible men—barely registers in the INS statistics.

Getting Through the Door

The media is entranced by images of paddy wagons packed with illegal immigrants, yet the fact remains that the majority of those who enter the United States do so legally. According to the logic of the Immigration Act of 1990, this means that they come for one of three reasons: to reunify families, to benefit the U.S. economy, or to maintain domestic "diversity."

The last of these is somewhat euphemistic. Congress, acting on the belief that immigrants from Asia and Latin America were "over-represented," enacted quotas for immigration from "underrepresented" countries. The largest beneficiary? The Irish.

Of the 700,000 immigrants the United States allows entry to each year, visas are given to 140,000 for their occupational qualifications, to 480,000 so that they can join their families, and to some 40,000 for "diversity."

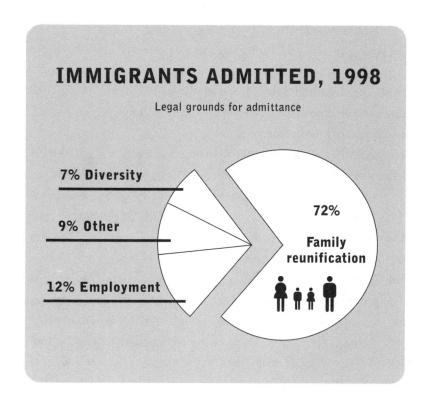

IMMIGRANTS ADMITTED, 1998

Legal grounds for admittance

7% Diversity

9% Other

12% Employment

72% Family reunification

MOVERS

Mixing and Division within America's Borders

Today, new regionalisms of race, age, and wealth are emerging. As big, coastal cities become multiethnic melting pots of recent immigrants from Asia and Latin America, whites and blacks move increasingly inland and south. In this, a coming demographic balkanization—displacing the old city-suburb distinction—is discernible. Meanwhile, the elderly population is dividing between the Sun Belt retirement havens of the affluent and the elderly ghettos of the immiserated aged. The "new federalism" and the decline of nationally administered social services may give rise to the most problematic aspects of these trends in migration. The communities in which the affluent cluster will be able to provide superb public services even as those areas with the greatest need will lack the tax bases required to provide good schools, public transportation, or hospitals. To look ahead without an eye on these geographic aspects of demographic change, to insist on only "the general trends," is to blind oneself to the fault lines of the future.

Imagining the City

Thomas Jefferson imagined that America would be an agrarian state: decentralized and self-reliantly rural. The small farmer, land-owning and beholden to none, constituted his ideal citizen. Needless to say, Jefferson, for all his vision, failed to predict the reality of the twenty-first century. While in 1790 only 5 percent of the population lived in urban areas, by the late 1800s the industrial revolution was pushing forward a rapid urbanization. Urban areas claimed a majority by 1920, and today fewer than one American in four lives outside of such an area.

Today's Americans, though, remain confused—or at least remarkably divided—about America's cities. To many, the word "crime" first conjures an image of a rundown city center. But "glamor" or "art" seems to imply urban as well. And when pollsters try to measure opinions toward cities, the results are decidedly mixed. In a 1997 Gallup survey, Americans ranked New York not only as the city they would most like to live in and as the city they would most like to visit, but also as the rudest, ugliest, and most dangerous city in the United States. (But respondents were sufficiently divided for New York to also be ranked as the third safest city.)

Even when a generation internalizes a leeriness toward urban life—as the Baby Boomers, the first American generation to grow up in suburban America, have—they still flock to newsstands to pick up annual lists of the best cities to live in. Magazines targeted at Baby Boomers, like *Money* and *Forbes*, rank U.S. cities according to a set of select categories, but, despite their air of universality, they scarcely measure the social needs or personal desires of every American. *Money's* rankings privilege the number of professional sports teams in a city over its racial climate or gay rights policies. Sometimes, it seems that "best places" lists are better measures of which cities have the highest rates of gentrification—the displacement of established urban communities by the rising rents and suburban cultures that newcomers bring—than they are sound advice about where one should move. Still, the lists maintain their symbolic clout. When Flint, Michigan, was ranked dead last, city supporters ceremoniously burned copies of the magazine.

URBANIZATION IN THE UNITED STATES

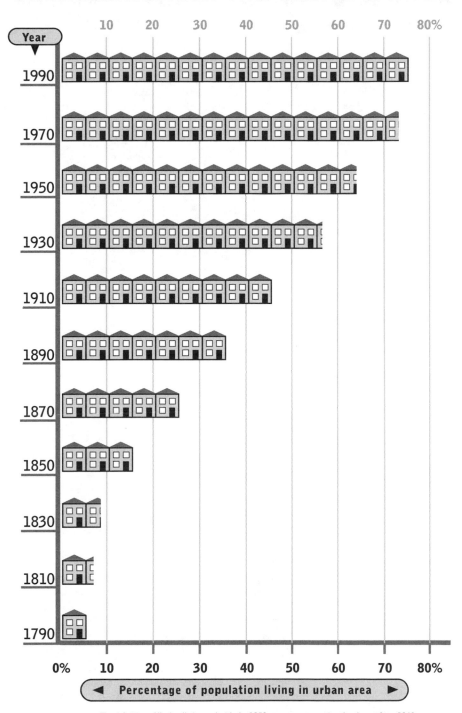

NOTE: The definition of "urban" changed with the 1950 census, exaggerating the change from 1940.

THE FACE OF TODAY'S URBAN GROWTH

America's largest cities, classified by their ethnic compositions and growth rates

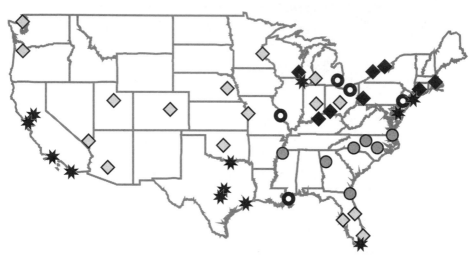

CITY GROWTH TYPOLOGY

The bars show the average ethnic composition of each type's cities.

· ·

✳ **Multiethnic high immigration**

| Hispanic | White | Black | Asian |

⬤ **White-black fast growing**

◯ **White-black slow growing**

◇ **Mostly white fast growing**

◆ **Mostly white slow growing**

0%   20   40   60   80   100%

Contemporary Urban Growth and Demographic Balkanization

Conventional wisdom holds that the nation's cities are shrinking as their residents flee "urban decay." While this perception is inaccurate, it nonetheless reflects a reality: native-born Americans, who have the cultural capital required to inform "conventional wisdom," have indeed been leaving.

The urban growth of the 1990s was fueled largely by new immigrants. While the two largest gainers—Phoenix and Las Vegas—achieved most of their gains from domestic migration, each of the next five largest gainers—Los Angeles, Houston, San Diego, Miami, and Dallas—registered a net out-migration of domestic migrants. Their gains came entirely from international migration and new babies, often the children of earlier immigrants. Indeed, many low-immigration areas, such as Philadelphia, Pittsburgh, St. Louis, and Cleveland, experienced population declines during the 1990s.

These trends suggest a new way of looking at the growth of large metropolitan areas. Cities like New York, Los Angeles, and Dallas are growing primarily due to high rates of immigration from Asia and Latin America. Others, such as Atlanta and Memphis, are experiencing influxes of both white and black native-born Americans. But cities like Seattle, Denver, and Buffalo are growing from white migration.

This new dynamic of growth has a strong regional aspect. Latinos and Asians are continuing to concentrate overwhelmingly in specific states and cities along the coasts and the southern border, only moderately spilling out into America's heartland. The Anglo-American population is diffusing into mostly "whiter" parts of the country, especially the Northwest and inland areas. And African Americans are returning in large numbers to the South. In short, America is separating into broad regions that will differ distinctly in their racial and ethnic blends, creating never-before-seen demographic divisions. The new demographic cleavage between regions will soon become just as significant as the familiar divides of urban—suburb and city—and rural.

Sprawl and Suburban Desire

The American dream, after the Second World War, came to include the possession of a large suburban residence surrounded by similar homes situated on half- to one-acre lots close to public transportation, work, and shopping. This desire for utopic suburban lifestyles led to urban sprawl—low-density development rapidly encroaching on undeveloped areas.

Suburban sprawl is a particularly American phenomenon. In European cities, residences in the city center are coveted for their proximity to commerce and culture; residents in European suburbs tend to have lower incomes than those in even the more downtrodden urban districts.

To explain America's unique and seemingly insatiable desire to sprawl, one has to look toward another peculiarly American fetish: the automobile.

COMMUTING FOREVER
TIME SPENT DRIVING TO WORK

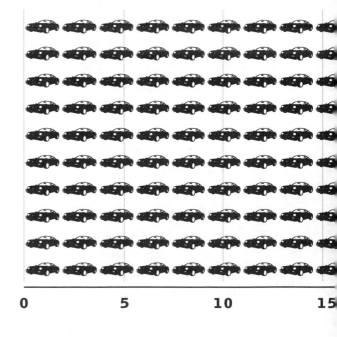

SAN ANTONIO			
PHOENIX			
DALLAS			
DETROIT			
SAN DIEGO			
PHILADELPHIA			
HOUSTON			
CHICAGO			
LOS ANGELES			
NEW YORK			

0   5   10   15

Only in America is earning a driver's license among the most important teenage rites of passage. Automobiles made suburbanization possible and are now needed to cope with its consequences. Between 1983 and 1997, the average round-trip commute to work in the United States grew 37 percent to fourteen miles. Today, metropolitan drivers spend about forty hours every year sitting in stopped traffic.

And the automobile itself can worsen suburbanite isolation from urban culture. Although many suburban residents need to commute to city centers to work, their cars also provide them a means of escape from the downtowns they tend to distrust and fear. And Baby Boomers—those with the economic clout to revitalize downtown areas—are especially adverse to urban life. When the commuting Baby Boomer does see the city in which she works, she often sees it only through the windshield on her way home.

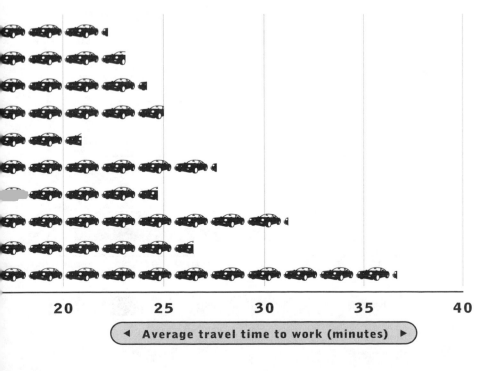

| 20 | 25 | 30 | 35 | 40 |

◄ Average travel time to work (minutes) ►

THE NEW SUBURBAN DIVERSITY, 1990

Hispanics are excluded from the white, black, and Asian categories.

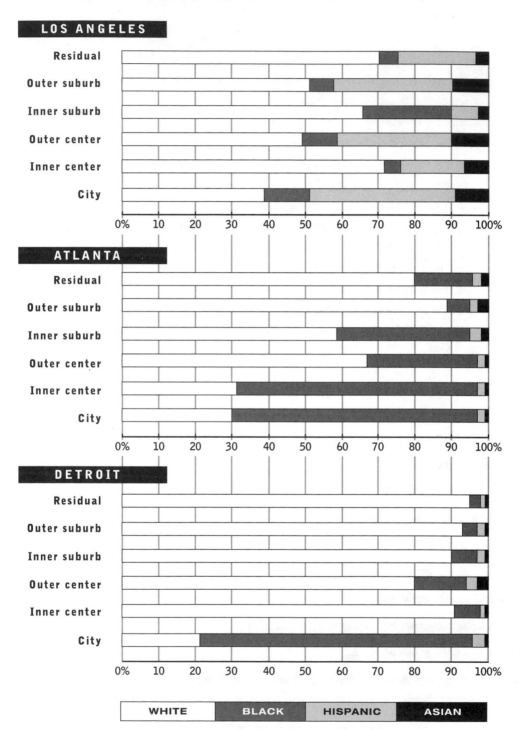

LOS ANGELES

Residual
Outer suburb
Inner suburb
Outer center
Inner center
City

0% 10 20 30 40 50 60 70 80 90 100%

ATLANTA

Residual
Outer suburb
Inner suburb
Outer center
Inner center
City

0% 10 20 30 40 50 60 70 80 90 100%

DETROIT

Residual
Outer suburb
Inner suburb
Outer center
Inner center
City

0% 10 20 30 40 50 60 70 80 90 100%

WHITE   BLACK   HISPANIC   ASIAN

Beyond
Black Cities and
White Suburbs

From the 1950s through today, much of America's collective imagining of suburbia—middle class, white, single family homes, friendly neighbors with similar demographic attributes (that is, white)—can be summarized in a single phrase: not the city.

But rigid distinctions between city and suburb have become less common. The old city/suburb typology fails to account for contemporary suburban growth patterns. Many inner and even middle suburbs are experiencing demographic dynamics similar to those of the cities. This is especially the case in some of the largest multiethnic metropolitan areas.

In the metropolitan regions of Los Angeles, San Francisco, and New York, many of the suburbs, as well as all of the central cities, would actually be shrinking if it were not for high rates of international immigration. No longer can the suburbs be seen simply as bastions of fleeing whites. The outer residential suburbs of Los Angeles, for instance, are barely 50 percent white.

There are, of course, exceptions. In greater Detroit, slow growth and enduring racial antagonisms have kept the divide between city and suburbs fairly sharp, with the city predominantly black but the suburbs more than 90 percent white. And the fastest growing suburbs of some cities—Denver, Atlanta, Las Vegas, and Houston—tend to lie furthest from the city proper, suggesting a continued popularity of suburban residence, especially among whites.

Multiethnic Metros and the Diversity Myth

The commentaries that flow from the pens of New York columnists and the mouths of Washington pundits spread the notion that the nation has finally become truly diverse and multicultural. In reality, though, this diversity does not extend far beyond the immigrant gateway cities. Both major new immigrant populations, Latinos and Asians, are clustering in metropolitan areas separate from the white and black populations.

Greater Los Angeles now houses one out of five Latinos in the United States. Los Angeles also ranks first in total growth, claiming 14 percent of Latino population growth for the 1990s. The largest gateway areas for Latinos—Los Angeles, New York, Miami, San Francisco, Chicago, Houston, Dallas, Phoenix, San Antonio—together are home to over 50 percent of Latinos in the United States. Cubans predominate in Miami, Dominicans and other Caribbean groups in New York, and Mexicans in Chicago. Most Latinos not in these gateway metropolises live close to the Mexican border and continue to build on large, existing Latin American populations. A similar pattern of concentrated growth has occurred among the Asian population. Greater Los Angeles, New York, and San Francisco, together house more than 40 percent of the nation's Asian population and share almost as much of its recent expansion. Chinese are a major immigrant group in New York, Filipinos are drawn to Los Angeles, and both groups have a large presence in San Francisco.

Gateway cities, in many cases, have now reached critical cultural mass. Instead of dispersing like most of the immigrant clusters of yesteryear, Latinos and Asians are remaining in their ports of entry, held by family and linguistic ties. While native-born Americans migrate largely in response to the pushes and pulls of economic conditions, immigrants depend heavily on local, informal job networks. This lack of dispersion is at once creating dense pockets of diversity and vast expanses of ethnic homogeneity. In the new century, immigrants will be introduced to American life in one of the several metropolitan melting pots—each with its own racial and demographic personality. Residents of the Heartland, though, will experience little of this new diversity firsthand.

THE DIVERSITY MYTH, 1998

Each county is classified according to which groups are present in proportions above the national average. Multiethnic counties have at least two such groups.

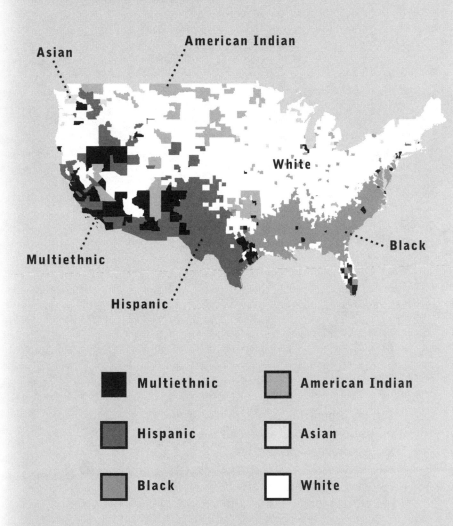

Asian

American Indian

White

Black

Multiethnic

Hispanic

Multiethnic

Hispanic

Black

American Indian

Asian

White

NET DOMESTIC MIGRATION, 1998–99

Domestic migrants are heading to the New West and the New South.

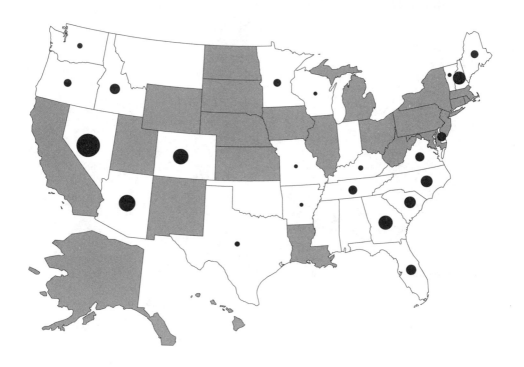

Circles proportional to net domestic
migration as a percentage of the
state's previous population.

(Shaded states had a
net outflow of domestic migrants.)

2.3%

1.15%

0.23%

5.6

Today's Domestic Migrant Magnets

While recent immigrants continue to cluster heavily in a few gateway metropolitan areas and regions, the larger number of domestic migrants—native-born Americans who move within the country—are dispersing from these traditional areas of concentration.

Many Americans are moving away from metropolitan areas to smaller urban areas and even to more rural parts of the country. Both residents and employers have found it more desirable and less expensive to relocate into other parts of the country, especially those pro-entrepreneurial and pro-technological regions that advertise themselves as economic novelties: the "New South" and the "New West." During the 1990s, this trend made Atlanta the number one destination for African Americans and Phoenix (in a photo finish with Las Vegas) the number one destination for whites.

But migration to the South and West is as much an attempt to regain the suburban past as it is an abandonment of suburbia. Relocating to these economic growth areas not only brings new employment opportunity, but also a return to the kinds of lifestyles that previous generations found before their home suburbs became less "suburblike" over time. The suburban life of the 1950s and 1960s can more readily be recaptured in the cities and suburbs of domestic migrant magnets—Charlotte and Raleigh-Durham in North Carolina, for example—than almost anywhere in California or today's Northeast.

And just as the suburbs were home to residents that were mostly white, well-off, and highly educated, the move to these new regions evidences a similar selectivity. Although both whites and more affluent blacks are migrating in droves to the new-growth regions, Latinos and Asian Americans are arriving in much smaller numbers.

5.7

The Black Return South

For much of the twentieth century, a hostile racial climate and declining job prospects following the mechanization of agriculture forced African Americans to exit the South. Industrial buildup in cities like New York, Philadelphia, Chicago, and Detroit created new jobs, clearly defining the endpoints of northward migration paths. The northward (and also westward) migration of African Americans continued in the immediate postwar decades, at the same time that many whites began to move in the opposite direction—to a newly reinvigorated South.

But for African Americans, the North's attraction began to fade. The early 1970s ushered in a period of deindustrialization and downsizing of much inner-city blue-collar employment, devastating Northern black workers. And despite the enactment of significant civil rights laws in the 1960s, the level of white-black residential segregation in Northern cities began to rival, or even to exceed, that in the South.

For the first time in many decades, the census measurements of the 1970s showed a migration back to the South. This trend gained momentum in the 1980s and accelerated rapidly in the 1990s. For the first time in the twentieth century, 1990's census surveys showed the South to have gained African Americans from each of the other three regions: the Northeast, Midwest, and West.

In the 1990s, Southern states attracted a higher share of African American migrants than of any other ethnic or racial group. For professional, college-educated blacks, Southern metros offer large middle-class black populations that provide opportunities for networking and outlets for political advocacy. For blue-collar blacks who bore the brunt of industrial downsizing in the North, a lattice of family and kinship ties is still available in the South. For elderly blacks, even more than for whites, the South is a likely destination. In the coming decades, thousands of retiring black Baby Boomers are expected to return to the same cities and states that their parents left to find work in the North—this time in far better economic shape.

REVERSING THE FLOWS

Arrows show the net domestic migration of African Americans between the South and other regions. After more than a century of migration north, blacks are returning to the South.

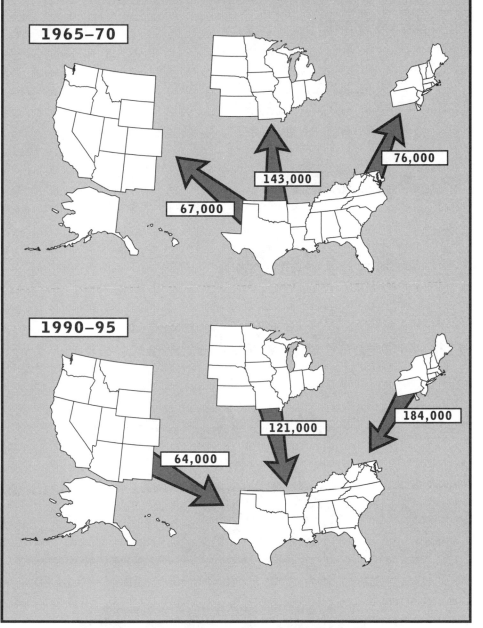

1965–70

67,000

143,000

76,000

1990–95

64,000

121,000

184,000

MIGRATION RATE BY AGE, 1990

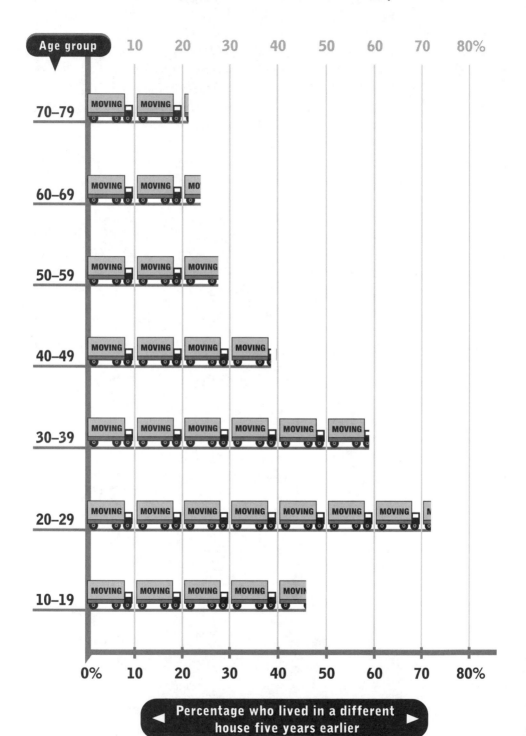

Percentage who lived in a different house five years earlier

5.8

The Young
and the Restless

Migration is a ubiquitous phenomenon in the United States. But the romantic image of a footloose nation of wanderers, willing to pack up and embark on a transcontinental pursuit of happiness is far from reality. The most common moves are made for less than glamorous reasons: to leave one's parents' home, to go to college, to relocate from a rental to an owned home or condo, to make room for expected children, or to cope with a recent divorce. In general such moves are across town or into the next county.

Long-distance moves are more closely tied to jobs. Likely candidates to move across the country are recent college graduates and those transferring between jobs within companies. However, the ascent of small businesses, independent consultants, and entrepreneurs should give rise to more moves that are not dictated by the restructuring of large corporations.

The different motivations for long-distance moves reflect the demographic groups most likely to make them. College graduates are 50 percent more likely to move across state lines than high-school graduates and move at more than twice the rate of high-school dropouts. College graduates are more likely to be in the national job market and involved in networks that provide greater information about other parts of the country. But high-school dropouts, in part because of their lower rates of home ownership, are more likely to move locally.

Whatever their education, young adults are the most likely to move. In any given year, close to one-third of all twenty-somethings move, as opposed to about 14 percent of late-thirty-somethings and less than 5 percent of senior citizens. Over the next ten years, Gen Xers and Gen Yers will occupy the high migration ages. While it's safe to say that they are likely to move a lot, the prediction about where they will move is less clear-cut. Compared with the Ozzie-and-Harriet households of the 1950s, these generations are more likely to put off marriage and follow their careers.

Technopolises: Today's Emerging Industry Towns

The fates of many major American cities have been bound to the fortunes of a single industry: Pittsburgh, for instance, was built on a foundation of steel; Detroit rode the automobile to fame, then followed it into decline. City centers were born around compact constellations of factories, then sprawled outward as populations grew. Today's high-growth "industry towns," however, are far more diffuse, and, it could be said, far less industrial. As computer and information technology became a major field of growth in the 1980s and 1990s, programmers and engineers flocked to a few hub cities—San Jose, California; Cambridge, Massachusetts; and Redmond, Washington. In recent years, high technology has made San Jose, once a mere suburban satellite of San Francisco, a major metropolitan area.

Technopolis growth has not followed the urban development patterns of yesteryear. Although there are exceptions—a "Silicon Alley" has emerged in Manhattan, alongside established media and financial districts—most tech centers are spread loosely around satellite cities and suburbs. Silicon Valley, for example, is a loose amalgamation of cities and towns stretching through California's South Bay area without any well-defined downtown—in essence, a nicknamed sprawl.

Because incoming engineers are predominantly male and affluent, dependence on technology-driven growth can skew a region's demographics. In some areas of Silicon Valley, the ratio of men to women is as high as three to two. Moreover, technopolises are gaining notoriety for their economic polarization. With uniquely high concentrations of millionaires, and even entry-level technology jobs sometimes paying more than $60,000 per year, many technopolises tend to have three classes: newly wealthy programmers, extraordinarily wealthy financiers, and an often impoverished service-sector working class that supports the other's daily routines.

THE TECHNOLOGY TOP TEN, 1998

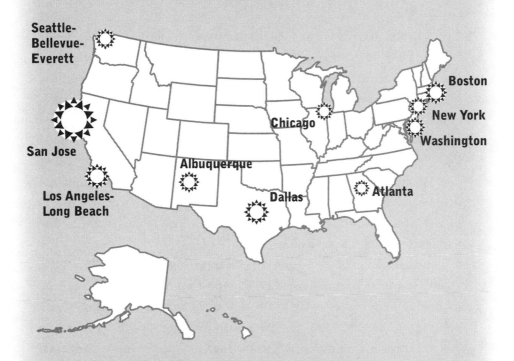

Seattle-Bellevue-Everett

San Jose

Los Angeles-Long Beach

Albuquerque

Chicago

Dallas

Atlanta

Boston

New York

Washington

Each of the designated cities was selected as a top "tech-pole" by the Milken Institute for being home to a cluster of high-tech industry that contributes a large share of national high-tech production.

Circles are proportional to this combination of local concentration and national strength.

Elderly Movers and Stayers

Certain states have developed reputations as retiree havens. Florida is particularly famous for its large older population, and the statistics bear out the distinction: in 1998, 18.3 percent of Florida's residents were over sixty-five (the national average was 12.7 percent). Only California, the most populous state, held more seniors.

Warm and dry Sun Belt states have seen the fastest rises in their proportions of older residents. From Nevada to Texas, the Southwest's elderly population grew by more than 15 percent in the 1990s. These figures can easily mislead one to think that all elderly growth is the result of waves of newly arriving retirees, but the elderly migration rate is small compared to that of the rest of the population.

In any given year, about 16 percent of working-age Americans make a residential move. In contrast, less than 5 percent of the elderly relocate, and most of these moves are local. Just over 1 percent of the elderly population moves to a different state in any given year. The migration of the elderly is less important for the nation as a whole than for specific "retirement magnets"—communities, states, and regions that hold special attraction for elderly residents. Small numbers of elderly migrants from a variety of places descend upon a small number of destinations where their impact is significant. However, on the whole, the growth or decline of the elderly population in most communities is less dependent on migration than on the simple "aging-in-place" of existing residents.

Elderly "movers" and "stayers" have helped create two classes of states with high proportions of seniors: magnet states—Arizona and New Mexico, for examples—with more new, affluent senior movers, and low-population-growth states—North Dakota, Iowa, and Pennsylvania—where more poor and middle-income older people remain, while younger people in those regions move to other parts of the country.

ELDERLY POPULATIONS, 1999

This county-level map shows that Florida and the
Southwest are destinations of choice for those who
can afford them. But the Great Plains have proven
to be a generational divide, with the young flowing
east and west, abandoning the elderly.

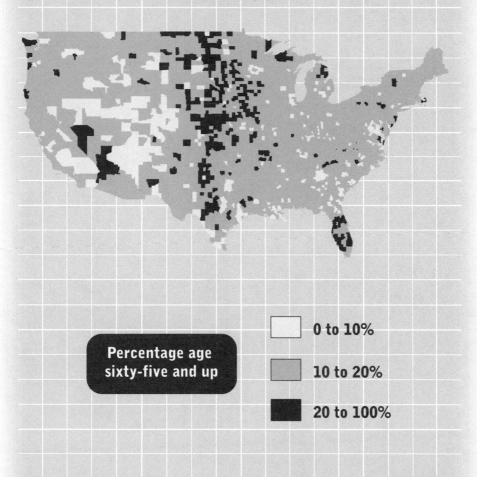

Percentage age
sixty-five and up

0 to 10%

10 to 20%

20 to 100%

CLASSES

Wealth and Poverty

The story of money in America is paradoxical. While inequalities of income and wealth are extreme, most of those with the highest incomes, and many of those with the lowest, consider themselves "middle class." The perception of an all-encompassing middle class does not, though, eliminate the connections between the production of wealth and the production of poverty. Investors and employers—the wealthy—live in an economic environment they have shaped by funding election campaigns, advocacy groups, and lobbying efforts. These efforts have led to the lax (and poorly funded) enforcement of labor law, fiscal policies that lower taxes on the rich while curtailing redistributive programs, and monetary policy that is used to maintain unemployment. It is a myth that poverty would vanish if only the poor would overcome pervasive personal inadequacy. So far, though, middle-class self-perceptions have been maintained despite enduring poverty and widening inequality.

How Americans Classify Themselves

America is a middle-class nation. This commonplace belief is not false, but it says more about the collective psyche than about the structure of income and status in the United States. Whereas many cultures have prized grandeur or distinction, America places its premium on feigned mediocrity.

Rich and poor alike profess themselves to be "middle class." The General Social Survey has found that when given a choice between "poor," "working class," "middle class," and "upper class," 45 percent of Americans identify themselves as middle class. This identification is favored above all among the most affluent, but even the poorest fifth of the population chooses it nearly one-third of the time.

This tendency to identify with the middle may flow from the American ethos of unlimited individual opportunity. Although there are many barriers to ascent, America lacks even the vestiges of an aristocracy. The poor can rise with few snickers at their ascent, and when the rich fall, there is no "aristocratic poverty" to fall into.

But the lack of social restraint does not make ascent easy or likely. Rich kids have a propensity to stay that way, and poor kids face stiff obstacles in the pursuit of wealth. The effects of rising income inequality on the way Americans conceptualize class may have far-reaching consequences in the coming years.

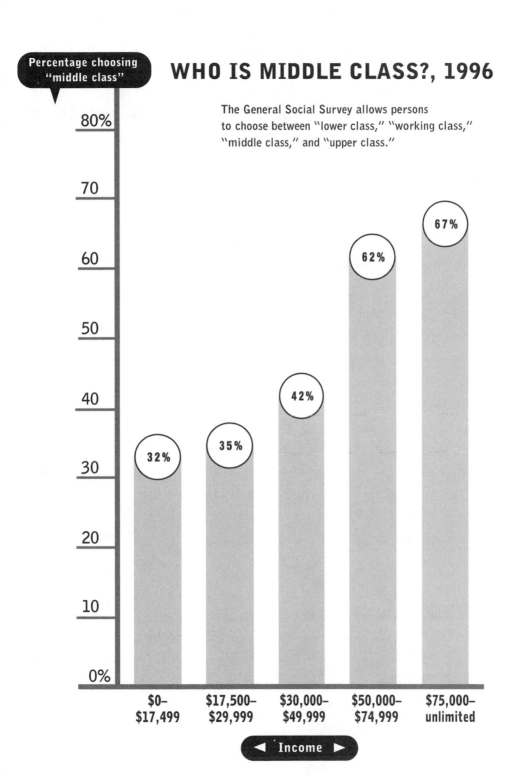

Percentage choosing "middle class"

WHO IS MIDDLE CLASS?, 1996

The General Social Survey allows persons to choose between "lower class," "working class," "middle class," and "upper class."

Income	Percentage
$0–$17,499	32%
$17,500–$29,999	35%
$30,000–$49,999	42%
$50,000–$74,999	62%
$75,000–unlimited	67%

◀ Income ▶

INCOME INEQUALITY, 1998

The chart divides U.S. households into five groups: the most affluent fifth, the least affluent fifth, and those in between. The mean income of each is designated. With the top fifth making over twice as much as those one step down the ladder, the inequality is startling. Indeed, it only increases: the top 5% of households have a mean income of $222,283.

DIFFICULTY MEETING BASIC NEEDS, 1995

A comparison of ability to meet basic needs by those in each fifth of the income distribution. Proportions who had telephone disconnected, could not afford a doctor, or were unable to pay their rent, concern the past twelve months. The period for not having had enough food is the past thirty days.

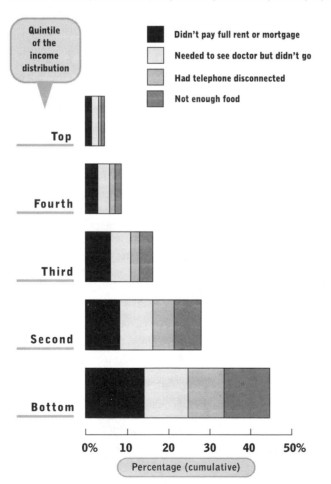

Quintile of the income distribution

Didn't pay full rent or mortgage

Needed to see doctor but didn't go

Had telephone disconnected

Not enough food

Top

Fourth

Third

Second

Bottom

0%   10   20   30   40   50%

Percentage (cumulative)

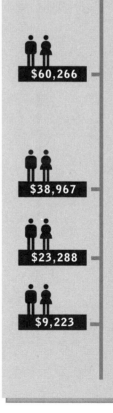

$127,529

$60,266

$38,967

$23,288

$9,223

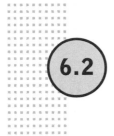

6.2

The
Rich-Poor
Divide

The image of America as the land of opportunity for all can easily conceal how polarized the U.S. economy has really become. Americans' economic fortunes are characterized by increasingly stratified levels of income. The postwar economic boom stretching from the late 1940s into the early 1970s truly was a tide that lifted all boats, but since then, the poor have been sinking and the rich have been getting richer.

The real incomes of lower- and middle-class households have fallen since 1970, while those of the top fifth have increased dramatically. Well-paying jobs have become scarce, especially for those with little education and few skills. Rising demand for skilled labor has burdened those who cannot afford additional education. Often, these individuals are forced to work in lower-paying service-sector jobs that offer fewer benefits and less likelihood of promotion.

In 1998, the poorest 20 percent of households had an average income of $9,223, less than one-tenth of the $127,529 received by the most affluent 20 percent. The most serious aspect of being poor is, of course, not always being able to afford basic necessities, such as food or shelter. But poor people also have lower rates of vehicle and telephone ownership and can often afford little entertainment or expenditure on their children's education. Factors like these reflect a social exclusion that makes it difficult to improve one's situation.

Wealth and the Wealthy

Little has changed since novelist F. Scott Fitzgerald quipped, "The rich are different from you and me." Of course, Ernest Hemingway's retort—"Yes, they have more money"—was not so far off the mark either. They have more money, real estate, stock, life insurance . . . But, returning to Fitzgerald, what are they *like?* The answer may be gleaned more readily from glamorous novels, society pages, and overheard five-star restaurant conversation, than from government statistics or academic studies. While the census will inform you of every number conceivable with respect to the very poor—age, cars, telephones, rent, years of schooling, children—about the very wealthy, it will tell you nothing at all. With wealth comes the prerogative of discretion.

The estimates we have are based on data culled from estate tax filings. As of 1995, 2.5 percent of adults had $600,000 or more in gross assets. These adults are usually male (63.4 percent) and married (70.9 percent of the men; 49.2 percent of the women). The women are often widows (30.8 percent); the men are seldom widowers (6.3 percent).

Between men and women who are very wealthy, the most significant difference appears to be the extent to which wealth comes from business. Men with net worth in excess of $10 million have 29.1 percent of their assets in the stock of closely held companies. The proportion for their female counterparts was less than half that.

Wealth as such may be a better target for envy than anger, but the facts about the distribution of wealth can be shocking. The wealthiest 1 percent holds 22.5 percent of net personal wealth; and, demonstrating just how concentrated wealth is, the wealthiest 0.5 percent holds 17 percent of net personal wealth. To put these numbers in human perspective: 1 percent of Californians are millionaires; 8.8 percent are in poverty.

WHERE THE MONEY IS, 1995

Each state's number of millionaires per capita
is designated in relation to the national median.

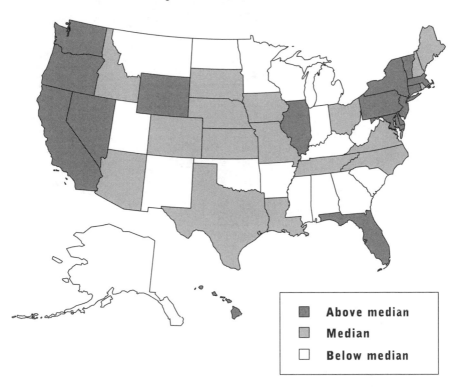

Above median
Median
Below median

THE MILLIONAIRE RATE, 1995

An indicator of social justice in America

	% millionaires	% in poverty
California	1	8.8
Illinois	0.89	12.4
Massachusetts	0.77	11
Michigan	0.52	12.2
New Jersey	1.08	7.8
New York	0.89	16.5

WELFARE BENEFITS, 2000

The map shows the level of Temporary Assistance for
Needy Families (TANF) benefits available in each state.
TANF is the state-run, federally-funded product of the
1996 "welfare reform."

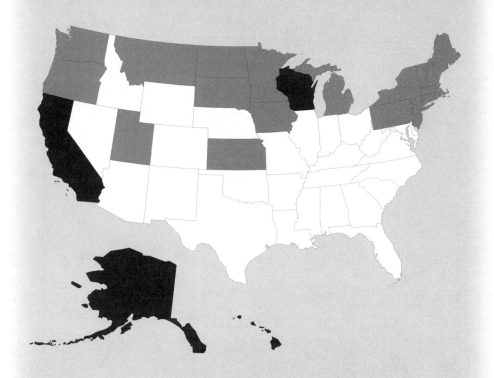

**Maximum monthly cash benefits
for a single parent with two children**

■ $670 to $923

■ $417 to $670

□ $164 to $417

Poverty and Policy

Opposing the provision of welfare has become a bipartisan sport, culminating in the 1996 bill that cut welfare spending and turned over its administration to the individual states. This policy shift has widely been viewed as an attack on the poor, or defended by referring to them as trapped in a "culture of dependency" from which they need to be cut loose. This is a dramatic shift from the days when poverty was seen as an unacceptable flaw in the American way of life, if not an indictment of the entire system. Poverty is now seen as a product of personal problems, not social problems.

The 1935 Social Security Act advocated social insurance and sought to protect the unemployed elderly population from becoming poor. Yet recipients of Social Security are not labeled as "welfare cases." In fact, retired groups receiving Social Security have become an influential lobbying group capable of garnering support for continued federal subsidies. On the other hand, poor mothers and children have been unsuccessful in mobilizing the resources necessary to lobby government for the additional subsidies needed to improve their general economic condition.

The Working Poor and the Production of Poverty

For all but the wealthiest of us, it is difficult to make money without working. But even with work, poverty cannot always be evaded: 41 percent of poor people old enough to work (sixteen years old or older) do so, but this does not mean that these people are able to find a solid job: only 13 percent have full-time jobs throughout the year.

The unemployed poor who seek work are up against stiff odds. Employers (and those who command the macroeconomic heights) are aware that if jobs are easy to find workers can demand higher wages for their labor, and that if there is always another job to be found the incentive for quality work is compromised. To avoid this unprofitable state of affairs, the Federal Reserve Bank attempts to use the nation's monetary policy to keep the unemployment rate a moderate distance from the zero mark. Of course, when such a course of action is promulgated, the edict is cast in the arcane obfuscation of high finance—politicians would prefer the connection between interest rates and unemployment rates to remain obscure to the recipients of pink slips.

Such policies are particularly harmful to people of color and immigrants, who are often passed over in favor of white candidates when jobs are scarce. In September 2000, the unemployment rate for whites was 3.5 percent, versus 7 percent for African Americans, and 5.6 percent for Latinos.

While profits depend on some measure of unemployment, those who collect the profits—business owners and bankers—have not stood out for their commitment to a strong social safety net. As the welfare state is rolled back, the well-being of the poor increasingly rests in the hands of the Federal Reserve's bureaucrats.

WORK AND POVERTY, 1999

The unemployed are likely to be living beneath the poverty line, especially when they are people of color. But even full-time work is no guarantee of a decent living.

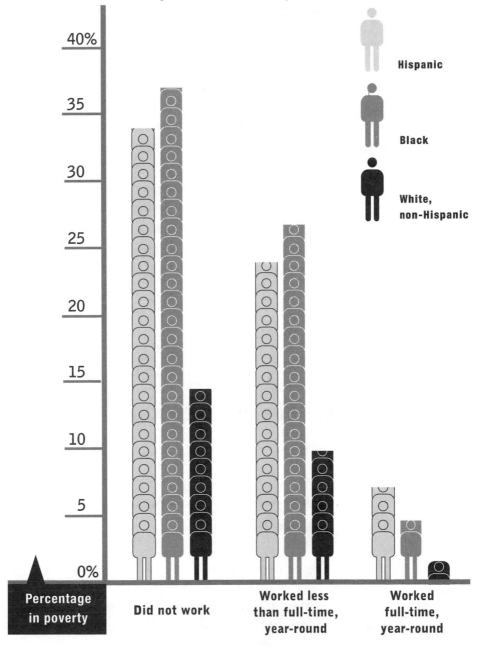

Hispanic

Black

White, non-Hispanic

40%

35

30

25

20

15

10

5

0%

Percentage in poverty

Did not work

Worked less than full-time, year-round

Worked full-time, year-round

Poor Beginnings

Today, almost one fifth of American children live in poverty, a condition that interferes with their ability to do well in school, limits the nutrition they receive while they're growing, and sets them back in life in many other ways. Progress has been held back by declining assistance from a government controlled by politicians who cynically claim that cutting off welfare to mothers will actually help the children.

The youngest children are the most likely to be impoverished. Of children younger than six who are living with a family, 21 percent are in poverty. Of those who are living with their mother but not their father, 55 percent are in poverty. For those children living with both of their parents, the likelihood of poverty is one-fifth as great as those living only with their mother.

The relation between family structure and poverty remains a matter of scholarly contention. Some argue that divorce and out-of-wedlock births are a primary cause of poverty today. Others argue that marital strife is often itself a result of the stresses and deprivations of poverty.

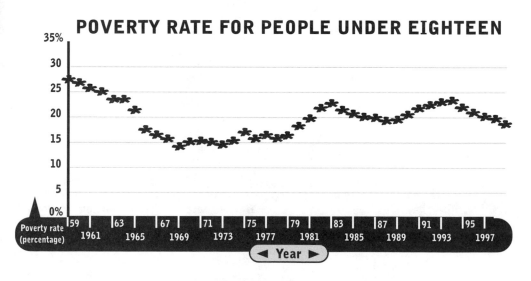

POVERTY RATE FOR PEOPLE UNDER EIGHTEEN

WORKERS

Labor's Continuing Necessity

Business gurus, policy wonks, and journalists incessantly bombard America with prophecies of a revolution in the world of work. Workers have moved from plowing fields to spinning yarn to pumping gasoline, and now, it is claimed, information technologies are bringing work itself to an end. Optimists conceive this in utopian terms: we will work only for creative self-fulfillment, unfettered by the necessity of labor. For others it is a dystopia: an overclass of the superintelligent and hyperconnected will become immensely wealthy off the computer systems they own or have the knowledge to control, while the remainder of humanity starves, unemployed, on the streets.

Neither of these stories is without its kernel of truth. Machines do, of course, replace people. But mechanization has never been, nor is likely to become, complete. When some workers get laid off, others continue to labor, with their heightened productivity providing the demand needed to create new jobs. So, with little hope for utopia, we strive together for less burdensome and more rewarding jobs.

Changing Collars

History has demonstrated market economies to be the most dynamic means yet developed for organizing production and labor. In the market economy, little remains constant from generation to generation, or even from year to year. Industries rise and fall, paradigms of management come and go, and the business cycle advances unabated. Indeed, many scholars believe that all the central themes of the American story are told by economic data. If so, the pace of the plot seems to be quickening even as its resolution remains far off in the distance.

One basic tension, though, seems to remain constant: how the American market economy can continue to grow beyond staple goods and farther from American borders, yet successfully diffuse the social pressures that development creates. In the last century alone, agriculture gave way to manufacturing which gave way to the provision of services as the primary source of employment in the United States. Craft unions, revolutionary sindicalist unions, and industrial unions have each made their marks on the political and economic landscape, and then seen them fade. For good or ill—and no matter how one chooses to value the market—Marx was right when he wrote that under capitalism "all that is solid melts into air."

FROM FARMERS TO MANAGERS

While particulars of ranking lack significance, the top occupations recorded by the census indicate the course of America's economic development.

1850

➤ Farmers
➤ Laborers
➤ Farm laborers
➤ Managers, officials, and proprietors
➤ Carpenters
➤ Operative and kindred workers
➤ Shoemakers and shoe repairers
➤ Salesmen and salesclerks
➤ Blacksmiths
➤ Mine operatives and laborers
➤ Sailors and deckhands

1900

➤ Farmers
➤ Laborers
➤ Farm laborers
➤ Private household workers
➤ Operative and kindred workers
➤ Managers, officials, and proprietors
➤ Salesmen and salesclerks
➤ Carpenters
➤ Mine operatives and laborers
➤ Truck and tractor drivers
➤ Dressmakers and seamstresses

1960

➤ Operative and kindred workers
➤ Clerical and kindred workers
➤ Salesmen and salesclerks
➤ Managers, officials, and proprietors
➤ Stenographers, typists, and secretaries
➤ Laborers
➤ Farmers
➤ Private household workers
➤ Teachers
➤ Farm laborers
➤ Waiters and waitresses

1990

➤ Managers, officials, and proprietors
➤ Operative and kindred workers
➤ Clerical and kindred workers
➤ Salesmen and salesclerks
➤ Laborers
➤ Stenographers, typists, and secretaries
➤ Teachers
➤ Cashiers
➤ Truck and tractor drivers
➤ Janitors
➤ Cooks

Women at Work

Throughout American history, the proportion of women who work to provide for themselves or their families has always been very high. What has changed—and has changed dramatically—is how many women earn a wage. After the rise of industrial capitalism in the nineteenth century, men increasingly sold their labor on the market. Most American women, however, continued to work without pay inside the home or on the family farm.

This has changed. Most Americans now regard the rigidly enforced isolation of women from the labor force as out of step with contemporary business and culture. For over a century, at any given time more than 80 percent of men have earned a wage or salary. One hundred years ago, only about 20 percent of women earned a wage or salary. Today, over 70 percent do. Historians will report that the entrance of large numbers of women into the labor force was the most profound shift in the demographic composition of U.S. workers in the twentieth century. Indeed, it could be argued soundly that it was the century's preeminent sociocultural change as well. Wage-

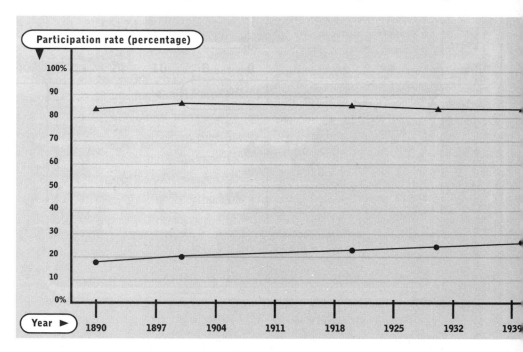

earning women in the industrial democracies today have greater earning power than women have ever had in the history of the West.

Many see the World War II era, with its tight labor market and "Rosie the Riveter" campaigns as the watershed period for women's first beginning to work for wages in large numbers. Such exclusive attention to the temporary upsurge caused by the war, though, risks ignoring how there has been a trend toward increasing labor force participation throughout the development of the American market economy.

There can be little doubt that, on balance, a woman's expectation to earn a wage has been liberating. The labor power of today's women allows personal and professional choices to be made that were unavailable in the past. Some worry, however, that the economic agency that women have gained by entering the labor force is culturally hollow. At the very least, the grand social transformation that many feminists hoped would follow after large numbers of women began to earn wages remains far from complete. Women working the same number of hours outside the home still earn less on average than their male coworkers and are often excluded from positions of authority, yet continue to bear disproportionate responsibility for completing household chores.

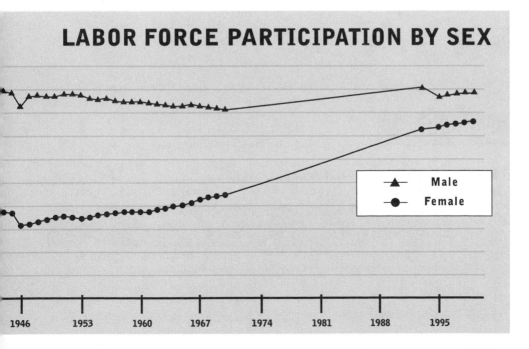

LABOR FORCE PARTICIPATION BY SEX

Male
Female

1946   1953   1960   1967   1974   1981   1988   1995

DEMOGRAPHIC CHARACTERISTICS
OF HIRED FARMWORKERS, 1996

Sex

▲
Female 16%   ▲
                    Male 84%

Race

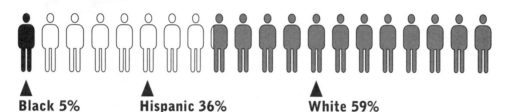

▲   ▲   ▲
Black 5%   Hispanic 36%   White 59%

Schooling

0–4 years	5–8 years	9–11 years	12 years	13 or more years
13%	20%	24%	26%	17%

From Field Hands to Harvesters

Driving through America's heartland, one sees endless fields straddled by irrigation systems. Occasionally, a mammoth combine might be seen rumbling along. The sight of grand machinery—though impressive—can conceal what is often absent from today's American farmscape: seldom does one see many people combing through the fields.

In the decades following World War II, labor-intensive farming methods rapidly gave way to mechanization. This decimated the ranks of both farm laborers and farm owners. Farm employment dropped from 6.2 million in 1953 to 2 million by 1993—less than 10 percent of the labor force. On the one hand, mechanization provided high productivity growth, reducing the demand for laborers. On the other hand, the high cost of new farming technology favored the wealthy owners of large farms. Many smaller farmers were forced to sell their holdings. Since the early 1950s the average farm size has doubled, as the number of farms has been more than halved.

These changes, while traumatic for some, were cushioned by a prosperous postwar economy. Manufacturing jobs were readily obtainable and often preferable to agricultural labor. Agricultural labor pays poorly—minimum-wage laws often do not apply—demands long hours, is physically strenuous, and can be dangerous. In 1997, the rate of death on the job per one hundred thousand agricultural workers was twenty—more than six times the rate for those in manufacturing and over fifteen times the rate for those working in the service sector.

The demographic characteristics of farm laborers have changed alongside the nature of the labor. The rate of farm employment among African Americans has plummeted, while it has exploded among Latinos, who now make up over one third of farm laborers in the United States. In part, this is the result of the westward shift of agriculture. The South once had the highest concentration of farm laborers, but farm employment in the South has fallen sixfold over the past fifty years, while the West's share has more than doubled.

7.4 A Postindustrial Society with Factories

The "deindustrialization" of America has been widely bemoaned by workers and industries seeking to protect America's manufacturing base. Deindustrialization, though, is less an economic transformation than a scapegoat for domestic stagnation. While some plants have been closed and some industries gutted, the United States' manufacturing capacity and total production continue to rise. This does not, though, mean that there has been no cause for concern.

The United States has declined relative to many other industrial nations. The Second World War made the country an industrial powerhouse; most of its allies and enemies were left with bombed-out factories and razed cities. But now many of those countries—notably Germany and Japan—have strong economies and robust manufacturing bases. By the early 1980s, the value of U.S. exports of manufacturing goods lagged well behind the value of those imported. To proponents of economic realpolitik, this "lagging behind" is an ominous portent of geopolitical realignment.

Manufacturing, like agriculture, remains vital to the consumer. But it is fast becoming as unlikely that a car owner has ever built a car as that a pork eater has ever slaughtered a pig. Production continues, but it is no longer part of most persons' working lives.

MANUFACTURING WORKERS, 1998

Even in the "rustbelt," many Americans are still building things.

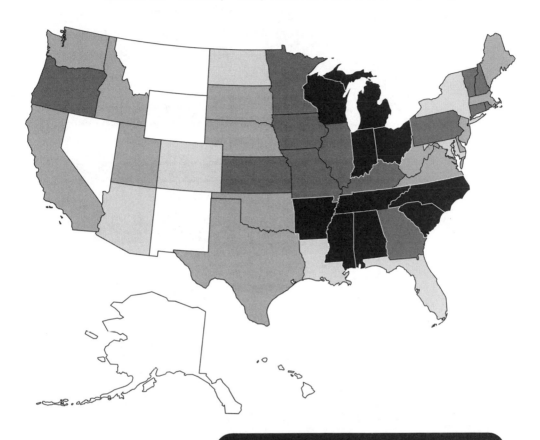

Percentage of all nonfarm workers
in manufacturing jobs

19.4 to 23.5 %

15.3 to 19.4 %

11.2 to 15.3 %

7.1 to 11.2 %

3 to 7.1 %

THE RISE OF THE SERVICE SECTOR

The proportion of nonfarm establishments that were service-oriented rather than goods-producing increased steadily throughout the twentieth century.

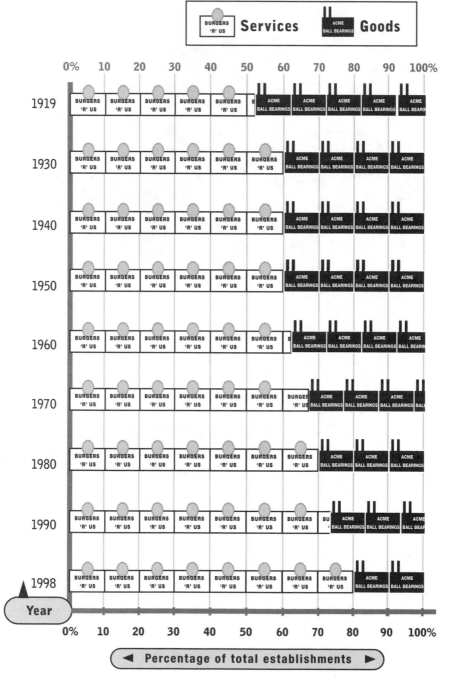

Year

◀ **Percentage of total establishments** ▶

From
Assembly Line
to Sales Floor

Alongside the last half-century's dramatic changes in the labor force's demography, there has been an equally striking transformation in the goals of work itself. The rise of the service sector is likely the most significant of these changes.

As the disposable income of the typical American rose—especially in the economic boom following the Second World War—the demand for health care, higher education, restaurant meals, professional haircuts, and other services followed it upward. By the 1980s, the share of personal consumer expenditures directed toward services had eclipsed spending on manufactured products.

This trend has had ambiguous effects on Americans. Many service jobs are poorly paid, part-time, and lacking in benefits or job security. But no one is only a worker: after punching out, we become consumers. Concomitant with the growth in service employment has been the advent of consumer society and its array of new purchasing and entertainment options.

A New Economy?

Low-skill jobs—cashier, salesperson, secretary—have traditionally dominated service-sector employment. Recent years, however, have seen the rise of the popular belief that a new kind of worker has emerged to surpass the old. Rather than merely maintain the flow of commerce, the "symbolic analysts"—corporate lawyers, software developers, management consultants—are said to drive the new economy with their technical knowledge. The faces of the most successful new workers adorn the covers of glossy magazines—very young, very smart, and very rich.

The beautiful people do exist, and they make great copy. But are they truly representative of a changing labor force? Although it is true that the fastest growing careers in the next decade are expected to be in computer engineering, computer support, and systems analysis, less glamorous service jobs, like physician's assistant, will be close behind. The expectation that the fastest-growing fields will eventually dominate the job market is as suspect as it is seductive. Job titles invented yesterday are almost certain to proliferate for a while. This does not mean that the average service-sector employee should anticipate ending her career as the "knowledge engineer" at an interface design firm.

The fact remains that more new jobs are for cashiers, retail salespersons, truck drivers (and, yes, systems analysts). Changes are afoot, but the new economy looks a lot like the old. Even many high-technology jobs are less appealing than they might seem: web designers sometimes make only $25,000 a year. And the cubicles of these "symbolic analysts" can be so small that they have sometimes been dubbed "veal-fattening pens." Moreover, occupations that begin as positions of authority and prestige can quickly be made routine. In decades past this was the fate of the clerk—a once respected managerial position is now often filled by temp agencies. As computers continue to automate office tasks and codify professional knowledge, many occupations of currently high status may lose their social luster.

CYBER-TRUCK DRIVERS?

Occupations are ranked by projected growth to 2008.
The first list ranks occupations by their **rates** of growth;
the second list ranks them by the **numbers** of expected new jobs.

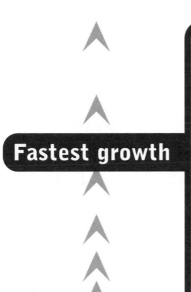

Fastest growth

1. Computer engineers
2. Computer support specialists
3. Systems analysts
4. Database administrators
5. Desktop publishing specialists
6. Paralegals and legal assistants
7. Personal care and home health aides
8. Medical assistants
9. Social and human service assistants
10. Physician assistants
11. Data processing equipment repairers
12. Residential counselors
13. Electronic semiconductor processors

Largest growth

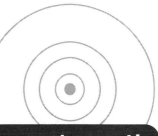

1. Systems analysts
2. Retail salespersons
3. Cashiers
4. General managers and top executives
5. Truck drivers, light and heavy
6. Office clerks, general
7. Registered nurses
8. Computer support specialists
9. Personal care and home health aides
10. Teacher assistants
11. Janitors and cleaners, including maids and housekeeping cleaners
12. Nursing aides, orderlies, and attendants
13. Computer engineers

7.7 Fighting for a Piece of the Pie

Never have a majority of American workers been unionized, and membership rates have been dropping since the late 1940s. Nevertheless, union membership is at least as widespread now as it was during the famous struggles for the eight-hour day, the right to organize, and the minimum wage.

It is invariably difficult to pinpoint the causes of a political project's decline, but the high levels of unemployment in the 1980s, the offshore outsourcing of many unionized jobs, and aggressive employer tactics have each played their role. The Reagan administration's decision to fire striking air-traffic controllers marked a turning point. In 1935, the United States passed legislation making the right to organize part of our social contract; in 1981, Washington would willfully disregard a striking union's demands. To many employers, the lesson was clear.

Organized labor's tactical repertoire has been evolving in this hostile environment. Unions have adopted campaigns to damage the reputations of

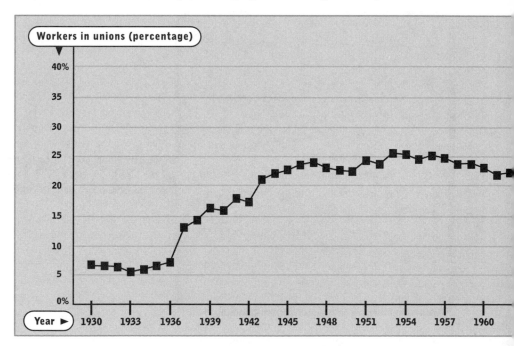

Demographic characteristics of union members

	Percentage of union members
Male	60.9%
Female	39.2
White	81.2
Black	15.2
Hispanic	9.1
Full-time workers	91.3
Part-time workers	8.4
Service	13.6
Agricultural	0.2
Manufacturing	19.2
Government	42.5
Other	24.5%

NOTE: Hispanics can be of any race.

union-busting employers, have formed coalitions with community organizations and religious leaders, and have made ties to students and environmental activists. All this has strengthened labor's hand at the table with business. Inroads are being made into the service sector and, significantly, into the public sector, which now contains 43 percent of union members. Unions have also become more female and less white. Gone are the days when a white man wearing a hardhat epitomized American unionism.

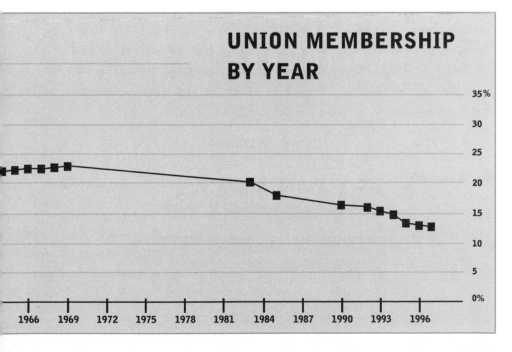

UNION MEMBERSHIP BY YEAR

The "Right-to-Work" South

Forming a union is always difficult and sometimes risky for the workers involved. They can pay a high price in employer harassment, time away from their families organizing support among other workers, and the constant fear of losing their jobs. Once a workplace is unionized, though, new workers are entitled by law to the pay gains, grievance procedures, and other benefits won by the union. To many workers who have struggled to form a union, it seems only right that future employees should be required to pay the dues needed to maintain it.

So, when the Taft-Hartley Act of 1947 passed with a provision allowing states to outlaw "union shops," organized labor took it to be a defeat. After its passage, many states enacted "right-to-work" laws allowing workers at unionized firms to opt out of membership. This practice is particularly prevalent in the South, a region where organized labor has long had a weak presence. In fact, the Taft-Hartley Act's passage impeded "Operation Dixie," a massive attempt to organize Southern workers. For this and other reasons, the South remains far less unionized than the rest of the country.

UNION MEMBERSHIP BY STATE, 1998

The South and the West have laws
less favorable to labor—and it shows.

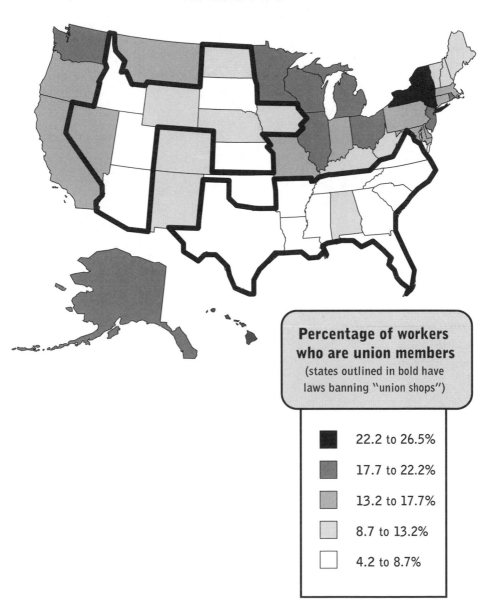

**Percentage of workers
who are union members**
(states outlined in bold have
laws banning "union shops")

- ■ 22.2 to 26.5%
- ◼ 17.7 to 22.2%
- ▨ 13.2 to 17.7%
- ▫ 8.7 to 13.2%
- □ 4.2 to 8.7%

FAMILIES

Renegotiating Norms

A quick glance at America's unceasing cultural debate over "family values" can readily leave one with the impression that it is only the second word that is in flux, as partisans bemoan or celebrate the transformations of the nation's mores in recent decades. Amid the furor, many fail to realize that the family itself has undergone a thorough and continuous renovation throughout the past two centuries. At the turn of the twentieth century, the typical family was agrarian, two-parent, and large. Ongoing industrialization, though, was already bringing about smaller, urban families. By mid century, the ideal family had become the nuclear family—one in which the father commuted away from the home to work for pay and the mother stayed at home to care for the kids. Some see the ensuing proliferation of family structures as a catastrophic nuclear family meltdown. For others, the new diversity can better be conceived as a liberating expansion of the accepted definitions of what a family can be. Whether it is a sign of progress or merely one more victory of a system run amok remains difficult to discern, even for those whose values may be clear.

Whatever Happened to Marriage?

Older average ages for a first marriage and higher rates of divorce and cohabitation have contributed to a popular perception that fewer people are married now than were only a few decades ago. These changes, however, have not been particularly dramatic. While in 1970 about 64 percent of the population age fifteen and older reported their marital status as currently married, by 1998 this number had decreased to 56 percent. While in 1970 about 3 percent of the population was divorced, that number has increased threefold in the past thirty years to more than 9 percent. Still, the proportion of people who have been widowed (7 percent) and the proportion who have never been married (25 percent) have remained fairly constant.

These statistics, however, fail to account for those who are currently married but have been through a divorce—the remarried. Divorce occurs in much more than 9 percent of marriages. Today, about 50 percent of first marriages and more than 60 percent of second or third marriages will end in divorce. Yet although divorce is more common than in the past, the duration of marriage before divorce has not shrunk.

So perhaps the greatest change in marriage is not whether Americans marry, nor how long their marriages last, but when they marry. Compared to the 1950s, Americans are marrying later in life. In 1950, the median age at marriage was twenty-three years for men and twenty years for women. But as women entered the workforce and attended college in greater numbers, the Truman-era imperative to couple early waned. In 1998, the median age at marriage was twenty-seven years for men and twenty-five years for women. When political push comes to statistical shove, the "benchmark" 1950s, with their low ages at marriage, appear to be more of an anomaly than any kind of norm.

MARITAL STATUS

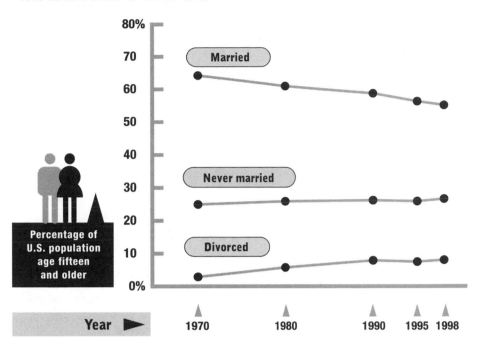

MEAN AGE AT FIRST MARRIAGE

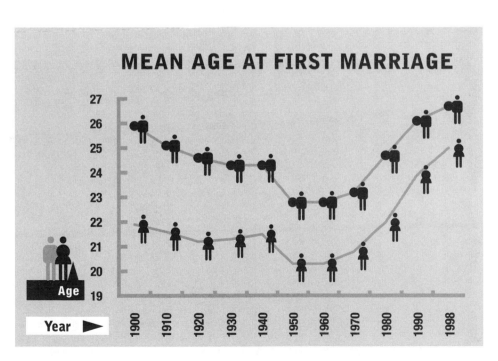

The Mythical Normal Family

8.2

When Americans, coaxed by the media and goaded by politicians, are asked to imagine a family, they probably most often picture a man married to a woman, living only with their two or three biological children in a single home. But studied examination of both the diversity of family structures today and how these structures have changed across time reveals that the "normal, nuclear family" is hardly the epitome of American culture.

And those Americans whose nostalgia pushes them to bemoan the nuclear family's "meltdown" from its high point in the days of their youth are often guilty of trying to recapture a past that never was. Only from the 1920s to the 1970s did a majority of American children live in nonfarm, two-parent households. Even then, less than half of the children in the States lived in a household of the "ideal" form—the homemaker/breadwinner fam-

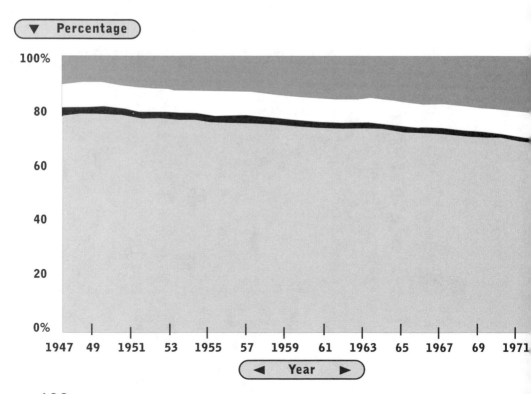

▼ **Percentage**

◄ **Year** ►

ily, a nonfarm, two-parent family where the father worked full-time year-round, the mother was not employed, and all the children were born during the parents' only marriage. And just as this ideal replaced the earlier norm of the farm family, the homemaker/breadwinner family has largely been supplanted by dual-earner and single-parent households. A century ago a child was likely to live on a farm on which both of her parents worked; today's child is much more likely to have both parents in the labor force, or to have only one parent as her primary caregiver.

Today, when breadwinners are homemakers, they are almost always women. Rising rates of divorce and nonmarital childbearing have lessened the number of two-parent families and substantially increased the number of female-headed families. In 1970, 85 percent of all children were living in two-parent households. By 1997, only 68 percent of children under the age of eighteen were living in two-parent households. Similarly, in 1970, only 11 percent of children under the age of eighteen were living in mother-only households. But by 1997, 24 percent of all children were living in mother-only households.

HOUSEHOLD TYPES

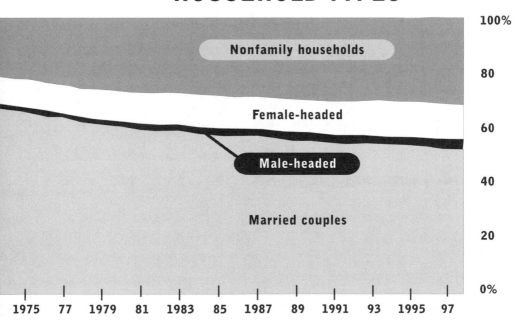

COHABITING COUPLES

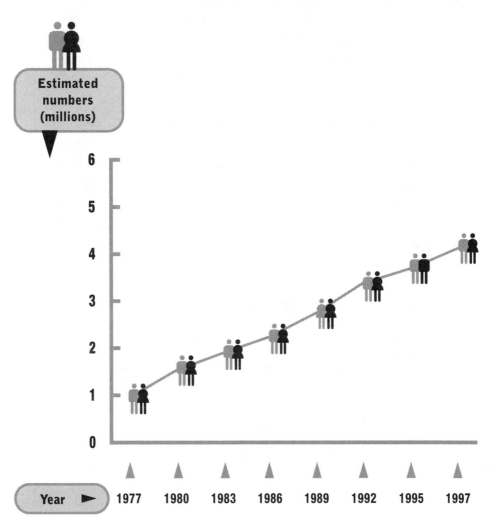

Cohabitation as an Alternative to Marriage

Living together without being married has become a more and more accepted form of family structure. The number of cohabiting couples has steadily increased over the past twenty years. While it is estimated that in 1977 there were about 1 million cohabiting couples, by the late 1990s this number had increased to about 4 million. The percentage of women who are currently unmarried that are cohabiting is slightly less than 20 percent. Cohabitation also seems to be more prevalent, and certainly more tolerated among younger than older women, so the trend is likely to increase in the coming decades.

Cohabitation is often a precursor to marriage. Approximately 60 percent of people who cohabit eventually wind up marrying their partner. Those who do not marry usually separate within two years. Although the majority of cohabitants end up at the altar or in the singles market, for some, cohabitation truly does replace marriage as a long-term living arrangement. Millions of Americans who are gay or lesbian cohabit, and many cities and companies have begun to offer benefits for domestic partners. Projections based on the 1990 census and other studies estimate that between 22 percent and 28 percent of partnered lesbian households and between 5 percent and 14 percent of partnered gay households include children. Of course, many of these households might prefer to be married, and only if same-sex marriage became legal would it be known whether, all things equal, cohabitation is truly preferred to marriage by so many same-sex couples.

8.4

Single-Parent Households

Single-parent families face tougher economic and social obstacles than two-parent households. Children who grow up in single-parent households are twice as likely to drop out of school, more likely to have children themselves while teenagers, and more likely to be "idle"—both absent from school and out of the labor force. Though many attribute these difficulties to a dearth of parental supervision or time spent teaching or advising kids, the predominant cause remains income disparity. Single parents have learned to expect lower income than two-parent families, not only because there is only one parent in the workforce, but also because the single parent is most often a woman, and hence subject to widespread pay discrepancies. Among African American families, which are disproportionately led by a single parent, racial discrimination compounds these problems.

Interracial differences in family structure, though, are not grounded in any recent "social decay." Research using historical census data suggests that the prevalence of female-headed households among African Americans is not a new phenomenon. Since 1880, African Americans have had higher percentages of female-headed households than whites as well as lower percentages of married-couple households. Yet, African American family structure also includes a rich tradition of extended-family support lacking in most white one-parent families. In recent decades, the disparity between the two racial groups has increased.

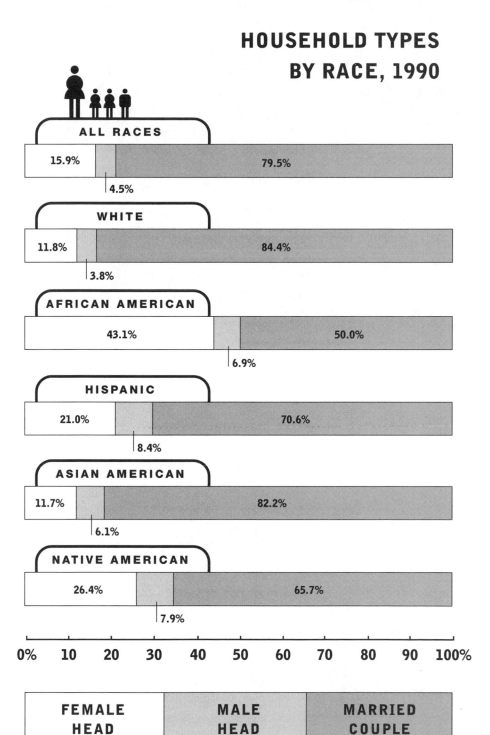

HOUSEHOLD TYPES
BY RACE, 1990

ALL RACES
15.9% 4.5% 79.5%

WHITE
11.8% 3.8% 84.4%

AFRICAN AMERICAN
43.1% 6.9% 50.0%

HISPANIC
21.0% 8.4% 70.6%

ASIAN AMERICAN
11.7% 6.1% 82.2%

NATIVE AMERICAN
26.4% 7.9% 65.7%

0% 10 20 30 40 50 60 70 80 90 100%

| FEMALE HEAD | MALE HEAD | MARRIED COUPLE |

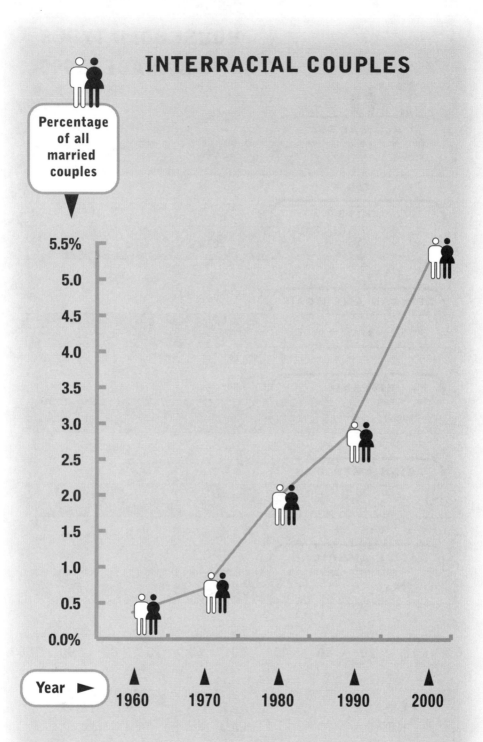

INTERRACIAL COUPLES

Percentage of all married couples

5.5%
5.0
4.5
4.0
3.5
3.0
2.5
2.0
1.5
1.0
0.5
0.0%

Year ▶ 1960   1970   1980   1990   2000

Interracial Marriage

8.5

Despite wide shifts in the American public's attitude toward interracial relationships and the raising of a constitutional bar against "antimiscegenation" statutes, interracial marriage remains rare. Today, interracial married couples still comprise a very small percentage of all married couples. Historically considered taboo in some regions, attitudes are changing only slowly. While marriages between members of different white ethnic groups raise few eyebrows today, marriages between whites and nonwhites remain suspect to many. In 1991, a mere 44 percent of whites and 70 percent of blacks approved of such marriages. In contrast, 4 percent of whites approved in 1958. By 2000, interracial married couples comprised roughly 5 percent of all married couples.

But even interracial couples can often fail to truly reflect the diversity of the United States. Whites tend to intermarry with African Americans in lower numbers than they intermarry with any other race. Between 1960 and 1990, there was actually a decrease in the percentage of black-white married couples and an increase in the percentage of white–other race married couples. During the 1990s, this trend began to reverse, as black-white intermarriage became more common.

Norms and practices of intermarriage differ starkly by partner's sex. Over time, the percentage of white male–black female couples has fallen faster than the percentage of black male–white female couples. Unlike a few decades ago, black male–white female couples today comprise a majority of black-white intermarried couples.

Growing Up
Is Different
These Days

Being a kid in the United States has changed a great deal over the past century. Not only have medical advances improved the chance of survival, but today's child shares his toys with far fewer brothers and sisters. In 1890, 12 percent of white and 23 percent of black children died before their first birthdays; less than a century later, in 1973, the figures were 2 percent and 4 percent. In 1865, the median number of siblings was seven, whereas in 1994 a child was likely to have two or less. The industrial revolution contributed to this drop, as the costs of having children increased and the benefits of having children decreased (child labor laws limited the amount children could contribute to the economic well-being of families, and a move to urban areas meant that food, clothing, and other necessities had to be bought). Standards of consumption increased as well, so raising kids became more expensive.

Children in the twenty-first century most likely live in households where the parent or parents work and have felt the effects of a sea change in child-care. Two major changes have affected the life of today's child. First, a lot more time is spent in school. Between 1870 and 1988, the proportion of days per year that a child spent in school quadrupled from 12 percent to 43 percent. Second, the time that parents spend caring for their children has decreased. In 1989, 48 percent of preschoolers had one parent at home full-time, 12 percent had two employed parents who divided the time to care for them personally, 15 percent were cared for by relatives outside their home, and 25 percent were cared for by nonrelatives. Although this is a shift from traditional forms of child care, evidence suggests that nonparental child care is not pervasively harmful.

CHILDREN PER FAMILY BY RACE, 1998

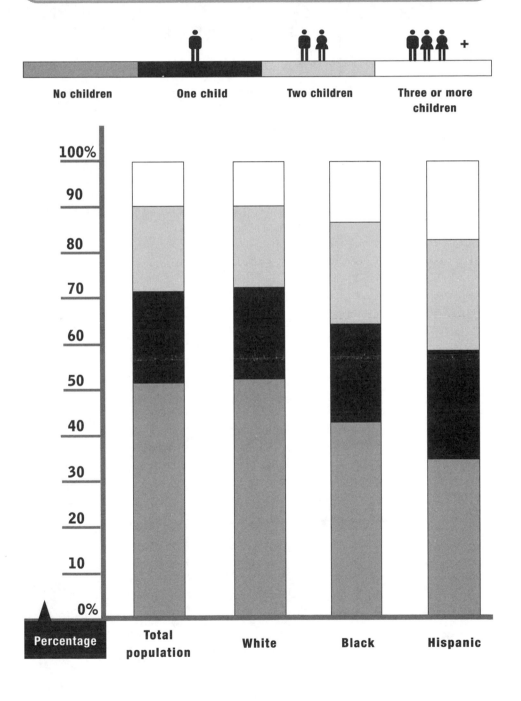

No children   One child   Two children   Three or more children

100%
90
80
70
60
50
40
30
20
10
0%

Percentage

Total population   White   Black   Hispanic

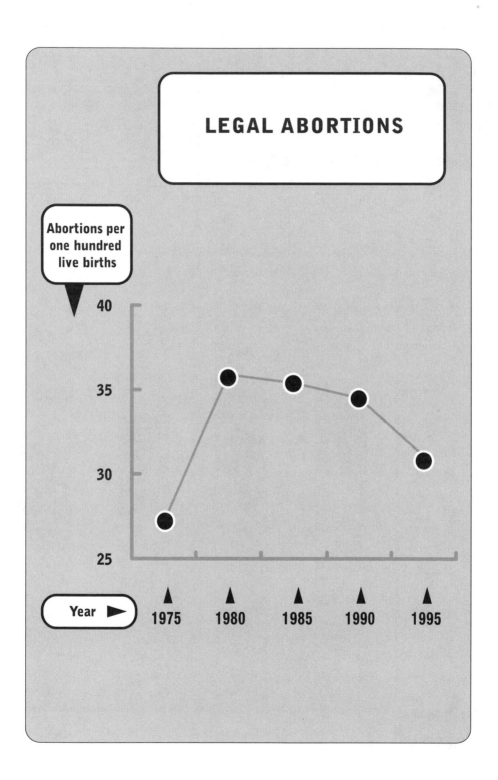

8.7 Abortion

Antiabortion laws first began to appear in America in the 1820s, and most abortions had been outlawed by 1900. Illegal abortions were still common, and often dangerous. In 1973, the landmark Supreme Court decision in *Roe v. Wade* made abortions legal on the grounds that a woman's privacy rights encompassed the decision of whether to terminate her pregnancy. While a majority of Americans have, since then, continued to support the decision, a vocal minority has incessantly protested it. Abortion rights have been curbed, as the Supreme Court has let stand laws requiring parental consent. (*Hodgson v. Minnesota, Ohio v. Akron Center for Reproductive Health*) and banning public funds for abortion facilities (*Webster v. Reproductive Health Services*).

Although the controversy over abortion may persist, abortion rates are currently decreasing without the imposition of draconian restrictions upon the procedure. This decrease is due to a combination of factors, including less-sexually-active teenagers, increased use of birth control, sex education, and more pregnant women deciding against abortion.

Teen
Pregnancy

The statistics surrounding teen pregnancy often lend indiscriminate (and sometimes unwitting) support to proponents of abstinence, abortion rights, antiabortion efforts, adoption supporters, and sex education. But one fact is clear: adolescents bearing children face a difficult struggle in a nation hostile to them and their children.

In recent years, teen-pregnancy rates have been decreasing. This decline can largely be attributed to three factors. First, teens that become sexually active are doing so at somewhat later ages and participating in sexual activity with less frequency. Second, when they do have sex, they are more likely to consistently use effective protection. Although use of noncondom barrier contraceptives has decreased, the use of newer, more reliable implant contraceptives has risen, now accounting for 13 percent of all teenage contraceptives. Third, more youths are abstaining from all sexual activity in their teenage years.

These decreases in pregnancy rates are widespread and can be found regardless of age, marital status, race, or ethnicity. Although non-Hispanic whites have continued to have the lowest rate of teenage pregnancy, the 1990s saw a sharp decrease in rates of pregnancy, abortion, and childbirth among black teenagers as well.

TEEN PREGNANCY

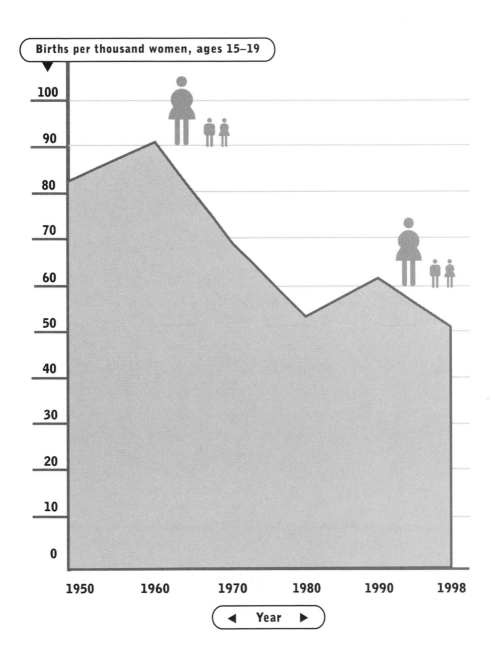

Births per thousand women, ages 15–19

STUDENTS

Schoolbooks and Skills

In an era when "globalization" has come to pervade political conversation, it is no surprise that international comparison has become the touchstone for debates over education reforms. As U.S. workers are increasingly forced to compete in a world market, fears have grown that U.S. schools are not providing the necessary skills. Several studies conducted in the past few years have confirmed that by the time they graduate, U.S. students' comprehension of math and science lags behind that of their counterparts throughout the developed world. The focus on international competition, though, has obscured the need to evaluate the desired ends of education. With the premium being placed on standardized test scores, the public debate over the assumptions and values underpinning such tests has mounted. Some question the "cultural neutrality" of the tests, arguing that they favor those who are white and affluent. Others question any system of education that can reduce the pursuit of knowledge to filling in small bubbles with number-two lead pencils. Some have said that standardized testing makes classrooms feel more like assembly lines than places of learning. But the attempt to maximize test scores continues.

Is America Behind?

For decades, rumblings have been heard coming from Capitol Hill as congressmen decry the inferiority of America's system of education. Sometimes, the worries are motivated by simple patriotism; Americans always want to be first. At other times, though, the concern is more pragmatic. As personal and national economic fates become more international and more dependent on technical, financial, and engineering skills, the comparative merits of the U.S. education system may in large part control whether American workers have the skills to compete in a worldwide labor marketplace and whether American corporations can survive in a global economy.

Recently, several studies have been conducted to determine whether or not the rumors in Washington are true. The results have broadly confirmed that U.S. students exiting high school trail their European counterparts in both mathematics and science. The Third International Math and Science Study, conducted in 1995, found that high-school seniors in the United States were among the lowest scoring in math and were below the international average in science. Fourth-graders, however, scored above the international average in both math and science. American students begin strong, but as they grow, the measurable results of their education fall behind those of their overseas contemporaries.

Although international statistical comparison might inspire competition and national goal setting, it does not necessarily indicate who has the healthiest system of education. Educational systems differ widely in their motives as well as their means. The baccalaureate system followed in much of Western Europe and elsewhere privileges test-taking ability over critical thinking and interdisciplinary skills; it should be of little surprise when students from these countries outscore Americans on standardized tests. A number of factors beyond the classroom also cloud the accuracy of direct scoring comparisons. Japan, for example, has a deeply ingrained culture of intense study that sometimes comes at the expense of the artistic or athletic extracurricular activities that are an integral part of American high-school life. Singapore's scores are often inflated as poorer students are economical-

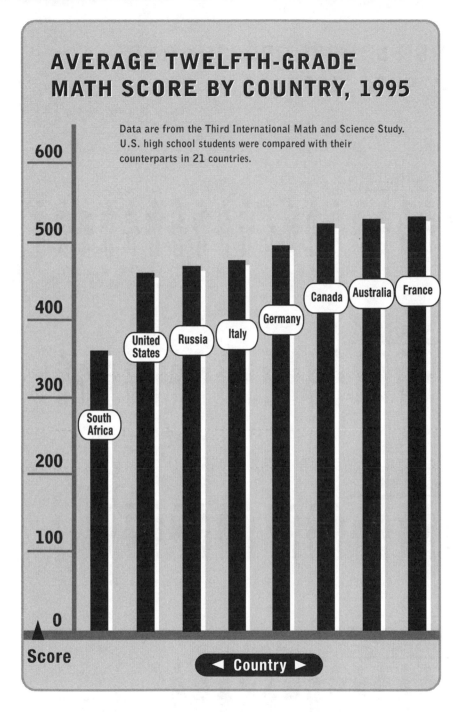

AVERAGE TWELFTH-GRADE MATH SCORE BY COUNTRY, 1995

Data are from the Third International Math and Science Study. U.S. high school students were compared with their counterparts in 21 countries.

Score

◄ Country ►

ly forced to attend schools in neighboring Malaysia, while Singapore's schools attract the best and brightest from the region. Comparative scores, then, seem to indicate the values and priorities of a state's educational system as much as they evaluate how well students are taught.

HIGH-SCHOOL DROPOUT RATE BY RACE, 1998

Percentage of those 18–24 years old who have not graduated and are not enrolled in school.

Asian

5% dropout rate ▶

White

9% dropout rate ▶

Black

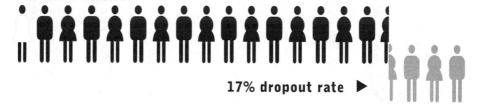

17% dropout rate ▶

Hispanic

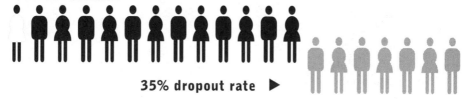

35% dropout rate ▶

Staying In, Dropping Out

The dropout rate for American secondary schools declined throughout the last quarter of the twentieth century. Between 1970 and 1998, the dropout rate declined from 17.3 percent to 13.9 percent. The demographics of dropouts have also changed. During the 1970s, female students were more likely to drop out than males. Often excluded from the employment benefits of a diploma and pressured to marry early, female students were discouraged from completing their education. Although female students are still less likely to obtain degrees in high-paying fields like business and engineering, their rate of attrition has fallen well below that of male students. By 1998, the female dropout rate was under 12 percent, while the rate for male students was 15.8 percent.

There are also significant interracial disparities in the dropout rate. Hispanics are the most likely to drop out, followed by African Americans, then by non-Hispanic whites and Asians. Economic factors can account for some of the dropout gap. Hispanics and blacks are more often in poverty and more likely to attend underfunded schools. Statistics indicate that low-income students don't perform as well as their high-income counterparts. For example on the 1998 National Assessment of Education Progress reading test there was a 20-percent gap between low-income and high-income students. Racial discrimination in education also plays a part. Studies have shown that African American students receive lower grades than their white counterparts even when completing work at the same level.

9.3

The Alternatives: Private Schooling and Learning at Home

Many parents, frustrated with the quality and direction of America's public schools, search for an alternative means to educate their children. Private schooling, albeit notoriously expensive, has long offered them one option.

There was no dramatic change in the 1990s in the proportion of students attending private schools and colleges. The percentage of students enrolled in private primary or secondary remained at roughly 11 percent throughout the 1990s. Over the same period, the proportion of students attending private colleges and universities remained at a steady 22 percent.

Yet the composition of private schools is changing. In the past, parents with limited resources to spend on their children's education would often prioritize their sons' academic fortunes over their daughters'. Today there is no longer a substantial difference between the share of female and the share of male students attending private schools. In 1998, about 9.9 percent of female students and 10.2 percent of male students were enrolled in private schools.

Asian Americans and non-Hispanic whites are more than twice as likely to attend private schools as their Hispanic or African American counterparts. In 1998, about 12 percent of white students attended private schools, compared to only 5 percent of African American and 5 percent of Hispanic students. Cost remains the highest barrier to entrance into private schools by students of color, but other obstacles continue to block the path. The disadvantages of largely underfinanced majority black or Hispanic public schools spill over into private-school admissions. A black or Hispanic student seeking to transfer from a public to a private school often must bear the burden of a transcript from a school with a poor academic reputation. And those who do gain admission to private schools commonly struggle to learn in a predominantly white and affluent schoolhouse monoculture callous toward their emotional needs or cultural backgrounds.

Recently, another alternative, homeschooling, once only a luxury of education afforded by the wealthy elite, or a necessity of isolated rural life, has

STUDENTS IN PRIVATE SCHOOL BY RACE, 1998

While the vast majority of students of all races attend public schools (or are homeschooled), white and Asian students attend private schools at more than twice the rate of black and Hispanic students.

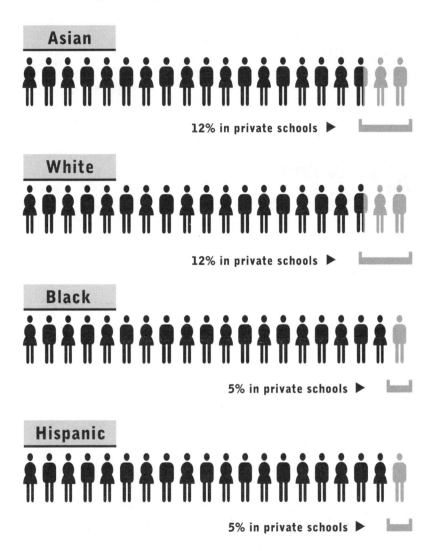

Asian

12% in private schools ▶

White

12% in private schools ▶

Black

5% in private schools ▶

Hispanic

5% in private schools ▶

reemerged as a mainstream educational practice. Parents have a variety of motivations for teaching their own children or bringing specialized tutors into their homes for living-room lectures. Although only about 1.5 million children, or 2 percent of America's precollege student body, are taught at home, the practice is growing at the rapid rate of 10 to 20 percent per year.

EDUCATIONAL ATTAINMENT OF WHITES AND BLACKS BY SEX

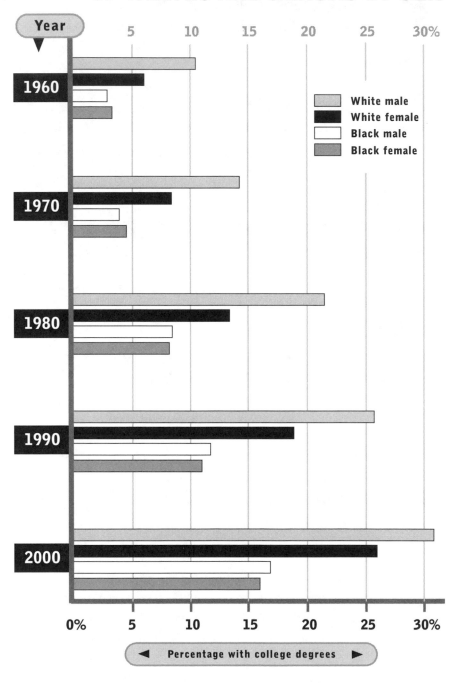

Year

White male
White female
Black male
Black female

1960

1970

1980

1990

2000

◀ Percentage with college degrees ▶

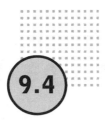

Minorities and College

Only in the last half of the twentieth century did people of color begin to attend American universities in large numbers. Since 1940, when only 2 percent of African Americans between twenty-five and twenty-nine years of age had received a college degree, the proportion of African Americans who are college graduates has increased nearly tenfold. For much of the past century, a combination of official segregation, economic inequity, and academic discrimination denied most African Americans the opportunity to attend college. Although many blacks did benefit from the passage of the GI Bill and legal desegregation, the largest gains came only after the legislative and symbolic victories of the 1960s civil rights movement. By 1995, 15.4 percent of young African American adults had college degrees. In the same period, the rates of college enrollment also increased substantially for other historically disadvantaged minorities.

The beginning of the twenty-first century, however, might mark the end of this trend. The continuing rise in minority enrollment has been closely linked to affirmative action and other policies that seek to draw more minorities into college. Beneath a rhetoric of fairness, several states, including Texas, California, and Florida, have taken measures to bar college admissions offices from employing affirmative action measures. Its opponents often argue that affirmative action policies, though perhaps necessary to achieve equality when they were first enacted, have today exhausted their usefulness. The short-term results of Proposition 209—California's 1996 referendum to eliminate affirmative action for the University of California system—hint otherwise. In the first two years after its passage, disadvantaged minority acceptance rates dropped by more than 24 percent.

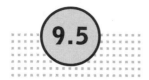
Enrollment Roller Coaster

School enrollment in U.S. elementary and secondary schools rode a roller coaster through the last half of the twentieth century, climbing and falling along with the size of the younger generations. As Baby Boomers entered kindergarten in the 1950s and 1960s, enrollment in U.S. schools rose dramatically. As the Boom graduated, enrollment in elementary and secondary schools decreased on a yearly basis from 1971 until 1984. Then, the first rumblings of the Boom's echo began to be heard; during the 1990s, school enrollment climbed rapidly and again broke records. Between 1988 and 1998 enrollment in kindergarten through eighth grade in the United States rose by more then 5 million students. As today's children age, this growth will continue up the ladders of education, raising student-to-teacher ratios in the middle and high schools. Later on, this trend will likely intensify competition for spots in top universities. Even today, enrollment has increased so much that some large universities have been forced to house incoming freshmen in student lounges or local hotels.

ENROLLMENT IN SCHOOLS AND COLLEGES

Number of persons enrolled in U.S. educational institutions

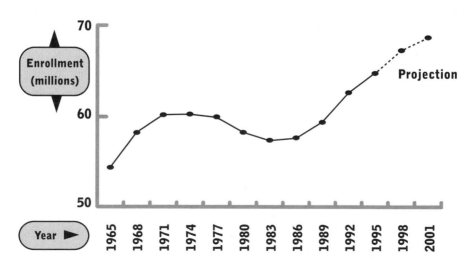

THE ELDERLY

Age and the Graying of America

The 76 million Boomer children—known to insider demographic circles as the "pig in the python"—are now moving on to the tail of that python. Numbers have ensured that the Boomers' business is America's business. The generation's senior members will likely shatter just as many stereotypes about "the elderly" as they have about the earlier stages of their life course. As the typical life lengthens, the ages at which work, civic participation, sex, and other activities should or must end are changing. Indeed, the threshold at which one becomes "elderly" is being pushed later and later into life. For younger generations anticipating their own later years, the iconoclasm of the Boomers will be worthy of attention.

What Is "Elderly"?

Americans typically consider sixty-five—the threshold of eligibility for full Social Security benefits—to be the age at which one joins the ranks of the "elderly." Needless to say, this standard is arbitrary. Public and private groups have wildly varying thresholds to define senior citizens: the Internal Revenue Service eliminates tax penalties for withdrawing from retirement funds at age fifty-five and a half; mandatory retirement ages can be as young as fifty or not exist at all; businesses begin to provide "senior discounts" to customers as young as forty-five or as old as seventy.

No matter what cutoff is used to define the elderly, wide differences exist between individuals. Thirty-five years separate the "youngest old" from the centenarians. Just as it would be improper to assume a person at age twenty would have the same characteristics and needs as a forty-year-old, so is it improper to make a similar assumption for a sixty-five-year-old and his or her eighty-five- or hundred-year-old counterpart. Many at age sixty-five are still working, have few health restraints, and are living with partners. Very few have not retired or are in perfect health when they turn one hundred.

ELDERLY ELIGIBILITY
A short guide to the opportunities of advancing age

50	>	Membership in "Over the Hill Gang," a recreational group for mature skiers
55	>	Discount for senior specials at Denny's restaurants
55 $^1/_2$	>	No tax penalties for withdrawal from retirement savings funds
62	>	Early retirement benefits from Social Security
65	>	Full retirement benefits from Social Security
	>	Senior ride fare on San Francisco MUNI public transit system
100	>	Birthday announcement by Willard Scott on the <u>Today Show</u>

The Widow Gap

Women dominate the ranks of the elderly population. A sixty-five-year-old woman in 1997 could expect to live, on average, nineteen more years. A man of the same age, could not expect more than sixteen. The difference in life expectancy between elderly men and women is not without social consequences. Today, widows outnumber widowers by more than four to one.

The widow gap means that elderly women require institutional care more often than elderly men. When one member of a couple falls ill, the other often becomes his or her primary caretaker. Because men tend to die at younger ages, women are less likely to have a spousal caretaker when they become ill themselves. Widows thus comprise the vast majority of older people in institutional settings. Nevertheless, most elderly widows live alone or with family members, and not in nursing homes.

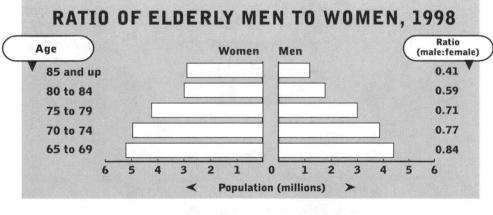

RATIO OF ELDERLY MEN TO WOMEN, 1998

Age	Ratio (male:female)
85 and up	0.41
80 to 84	0.59
75 to 79	0.71
70 to 74	0.77
65 to 69	0.84

◄ Population (millions) ►

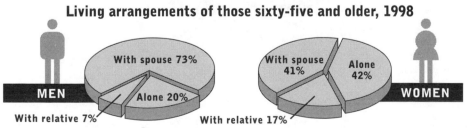

Living arrangements of those sixty-five and older, 1998

MEN: With spouse 73%, Alone 20%, With relative 7%

WOMEN: With spouse 41%, Alone 42%, With relative 17%

PROJECTED RACIAL COMPOSITION OF THE ELDERLY, 2040

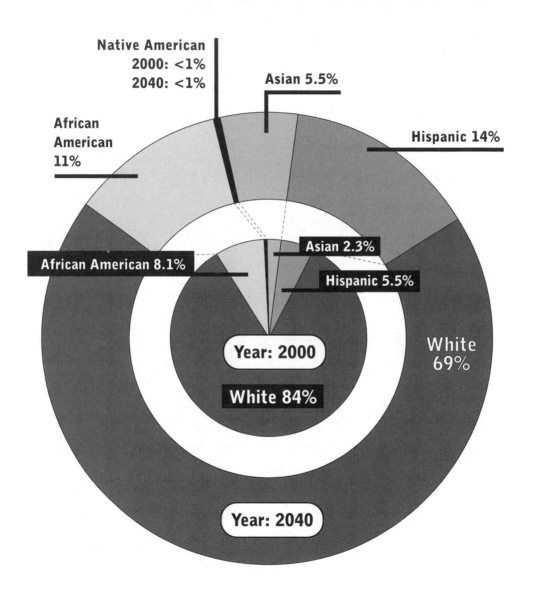

Native American
2000: <1%
2040: <1%

Asian 5.5%

African
American
11%

Hispanic 14%

African American 8.1%

Asian 2.3%

Hispanic 5.5%

Year: 2000

White 84%

White
69%

Year: 2040

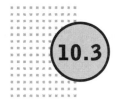

The Last White Majority?

The population of older Americans is overwhelmingly white and European. And the second-largest group is non-Hispanic African American. The composition of the elderly population is a reflection of the past, when most immigrants were of European descent and native-born residents were predominately white or African American. However, if birth, death, and immigration rates continue at projected rates, by 2040 Latinos will be the second-largest group of elderly, with 14 percent of the total, while African Americans will follow with 11 percent.

Although the high proportion of elderly whites is due in large part to their greater numbers at birth, it is also the result of higher death rates among many people of color. Non-Hispanic white and Hispanic children born in 1999 have substantially higher life expectancies than African American children.

As the elderly population mushrooms, younger America will become less white; the generation gap will in many ways become a racial gap as well. In 2060, 27 percent of the total population is projected to be Hispanic, 13 percent African American, and 10 percent Asian. As older whites and younger people of color compete for the same social-service dollars, the already divisive conflicts about the future of welfare, health care, and Social Security are likely to become even more polarized than they are today.

Elderly Poverty and the Weight of History

Social Security has reduced the level of poverty in the elderly population. Although older people are less likely to be impoverished than children, they are still more likely to be impoverished than people of working age. Many of the same factors that are linked to poverty in the population as a whole are linked to poverty in the elderly population: being a person of color, being a woman, living in a central city or rural area, and living in a Southern state.

Racial differences in elderly-poverty rates—7.6 percent of non-Hispanic whites, 22.7 percent of African Americans, 20.4 percent of Hispanics in 1999—are striking. Elderly people of color perhaps bear the heaviest burden of America's history of discrimination. Today's older Americans came of age when school segregation, Jim Crow, and employment discrimination were still in full force. In 1960, 45 percent of white women and 42 percent of white men were high-school graduates. That same year, only 18 percent of black men and 22 percent of black women had finished high school.

There may be hope that America has begun to surpass its track record. Poverty rates between 1980 and 1998 fell faster for elderly people than for those in the age range between eighteen and sixty-four. However, the rates fell faster for white seniors than for people of color. Despite rising educational attainment for elderly people of color, their standard of living continues to lag behind that of whites.

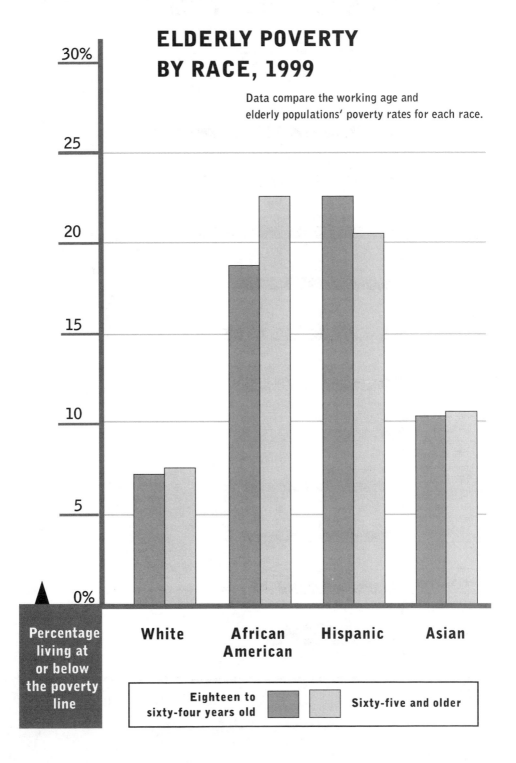

ELDERLY POVERTY BY RACE, 1999

Data compare the working age and
elderly populations' poverty rates for each race.

Percentage living at or below the poverty line

White   African American   Hispanic   Asian

Eighteen to sixty-four years old   Sixty-five and older

MEDIAN AGE AT RETIREMENT BY SEX

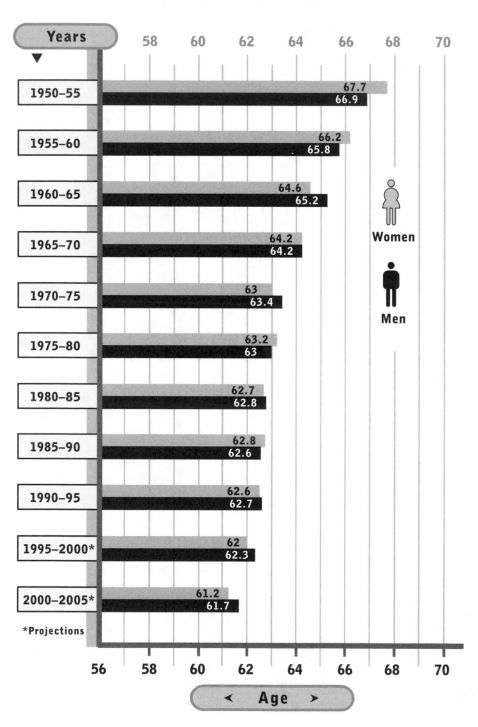

Years	Women	Men
1950–55	67.7	66.9
1955–60	66.2	65.8
1960–65	64.6	65.2
1965–70	64.2	64.2
1970–75	63	63.4
1975–80	63.2	63
1980–85	62.7	62.8
1985–90	62.8	62.6
1990–95	62.6	62.7
1995–2000*	62	62.3
2000–2005*	61.2	61.7

*Projections

‹ Age ›

10.5

From Work to Retirement and Back

A prolonged retirement is a relatively new concept to industrialized societies. Prior to the advent of public and private retirement pensions, it was up to individuals to accumulate enough wealth to support themselves later in life or to rely upon family and community resources. In 1900, over 65 percent of older men were in the labor force. By the end of the century, that proportion had dropped to about 13 percent. On the other hand, older women in 1900 held jobs only about 8 percent of the time. The proportion rose to about a quarter by the middle of the century, but had returned to its previous level by 2000.

The Social Security system has been integral to older workers' drop in labor force participation. In 1996, the older population received 40 percent of its income from Social Security. For many years, the system had incentives that encouraged workers to retire by age sixty-five. In fact, until changes were instituted in 2000, Social Security recipients sixty-five and older had their benefits reduced by $1 for each $3 they earned in wages, effectively a 33 percent tax on recipients. In 1960, 4.6 percent of working Americans were sixty-five or older. By 1998, only 2.8 percent were.

Where the Boomers Will Retire

While the nation's elderly population will have grown 80 percent by 2025, in many areas elderly numbers will have grown at an even faster pace. Most growth will occur as Boomers in the Sun Belt and suburbs age without leaving the communities in which they have worked and raised families. This aging-in-place will be the dominant force behind regional elderly population growth in most of the United States.

Some areas, though, will grow much faster than others. By 2025, Utah's elderly population is projected to be 2.4 times what it is today. And Utah will be merely the leader of a swath of Western states that have begun to draw Boomers from elsewhere in the country. The graying of some of these states, especially Arizona and Nevada, will come in a compound pattern, as they gain both from residents aging in place and by attracting retirees from other parts of the country. The same pattern of elderly growth will be experienced in the Atlantic southeast and Texas.

The second tier of rapidly graying states includes most of the rest of the South, plus California, Hawaii, and the amenity-rich New England retirement magnets of Vermont and New Hampshire. At the other extreme is a band of old industrial states stretching westward from Massachusetts through Illinois that have already lost large numbers of their Baby Boomers to other regions of the country. Yet even these states will experience considerable growth in their senior populations—38 percent in New York, 60 percent in West Virginia—over the next twenty-five years.

Not all of this growth in the elderly population will come from advantaged segments of the "yuppie elderly." Baby Boomers are privileged in many respects: high educational attainment, large preretirement assets, and high levels of health and life expectancy. Yet they have always exhibited wide inequalities as well. Locally, each segment of this generation will likely reside in different suburban and inner-city communities. Still, many of the "yuppie elderly" will engage in long-distance retirement migration—gravitating to high-amenity regions as states and communities compete to attract this lucrative group.

THE SENIOR EXPLOSION'S REGIONAL ASPECT

Projected percentage increase of age sixty-five-and-over population from 2000 to 2025

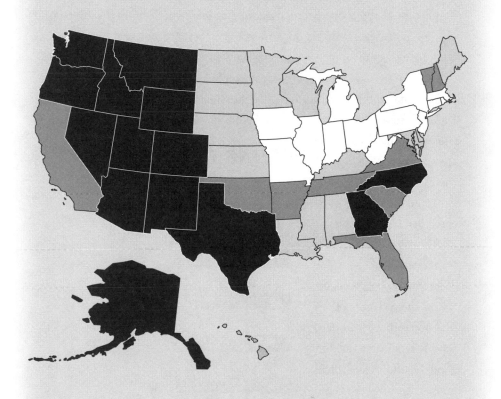

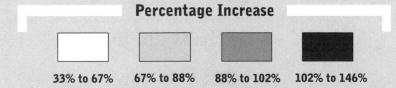

Percentage Increase

| 33% to 67% | 67% to 88% | 88% to 102% | 102% to 146% |

How to Stay Healthy

In 1995, more than 50 percent of persons sixty-five and older and about 70 percent of those eighty and older had at least one form of disability. And chronic illnesses—arthritis, hypertension, heart disease—are often seen as inevitable facts of aging.

Conditions like these can be extremely expensive to treat. Insurance, office visits, and medical supplies create enormous out-of-pocket expenses. In 1997, seniors spent an average of $2,855 on this type of expense. While those under sixty-five spend about 4 percent of their income on health care, the elderly, on average, spend 12 percent.

Although health is an important concern for older persons, the majority of them—more than 60 percent in 1996—report that they are in good health. As medical knowledge has advanced, more older Americans are enjoying active, healthy lives.

PAYING FOR LIFE

National health-care expenditures as percentage of U.S. gross domestic product

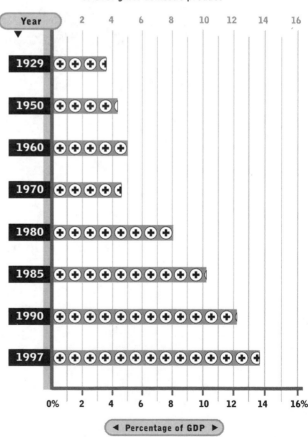

| Year | 1929 | 1950 | 1960 | 1970 | 1980 | 1985 | 1990 | 1997 |

◀ Percentage of GDP ▶

Neglected Violence

10.8

The elderly are not immune from suffering at the hands of others. But neither the traditional picture of the senior victim of violence—the little old lady whose purse has been stolen by an anonymous thug—nor its modern revision—the elderly couple defrauded by a swindling opportunist—is an accurate representation of the kind of crimes that threaten older Americans most often.

Instead, the primary source of violence against the elderly is neglect and abuse at the hands of their caregivers, most often relatives entrusted with the care of their older kin. In 1991, about 450,000 older Americans were the victims of abuse or neglect. Elderly women are more likely to be abused than men. Forms of abuse of the elderly can be physical, sexual, financial, or psychological. Forms of neglect include improper medical care and treatment, isolation, and malnutrition. Almost nine out of ten known perpetrators are family members; two out of three are adult children or spouses. It is perhaps unsurprising, then, that only about 16 percent of abuse cases are reported to an adult protective service agency.

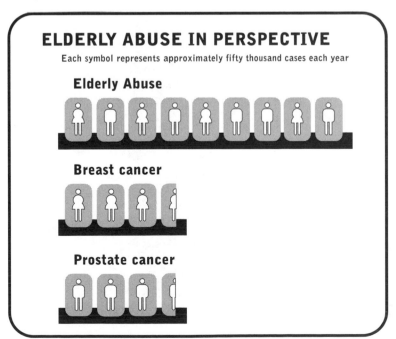

ELDERLY ABUSE IN PERSPECTIVE

Each symbol represents approximately fifty thousand cases each year

Elderly Abuse

Breast cancer

Prostate cancer

THE HEALTHY

Illness and Well-Being

In the course of the twentieth century, infant mortality rates plunged and life expectancy skyrocketed. Today, Americans' life expectancies are among the highest in the world, and those lives are among the healthiest. While the twentieth century witnessed an expansion of the role of medicine in Americans' lives, "healthiness" remains a subjective matter; although chemicals and compounds determine what happens inside our bodies, social institutions determine what we believe about how we should feel. Some shifts in social beliefs have certainly been for the better—disabled Americans now receive protection from needless job discrimination. But others are more questionable—low-level mental illnesses, in some subcultures, seem to have progressed from stigmatized to chic.

Americans seem more likely to doubt their health. Despite the fact that Americans' insides really are in better shape than they used to be, they refuse to believe it. In fact, they are slightly less likely to report today that they are in "good health" than they were forty years ago. Finally, although Americans might be healthy, most doubt whether the system that maintains that health is in such good shape—tens of millions in the United States have no insurance. And as the focus shifts away from the care available to affluent communities, the diagnosis goes from serious to critical.

American Lives: Long and Healthy

With a life expectancy of 76.5 years, Americans live longer than most of the world's population. And Americans pass most of their years in good health. The World Health Organization determines "healthy-life expectancy" by subtracting years from the expected life span to account for the duration and severity of ill health. Under this measure, the United States, with a healthy-life expectancy of 70 years, places in the top 15 percent of the world's countries.

Even within the United States, however, expected longevity varies significantly. With a life expectancy of 73.6 years, men live 5.8 years less than women. Likewise, life expectancy varies between racial and ethnic groups. While whites live for 74.7 years on average, life expectancy among African Americans is only 68.3.

Women live longer, in part, because they have tended to smoke less and have been less likely to fight in wars. However, as women's rates of tobacco and alcohol consumption approach those of the male population, this longevity gap is expected to close. Hence, it has been said that a tragic irony of gender equality may be that as women adopt practices once reserved for men, they are more likely to die like men. (The opposite, though, is a bit more accurate; as American men abandon cigarettes and history lets them avoid service in major wars, they are more likely to live as women have—longer.)

Homicide and HIV—top killers for blacks, but not for whites or Asians—in part explain the longevity gaps between the races. Both of these hazards tend to claim young lives, thus dragging down the average life span more than the afflictions of old age.

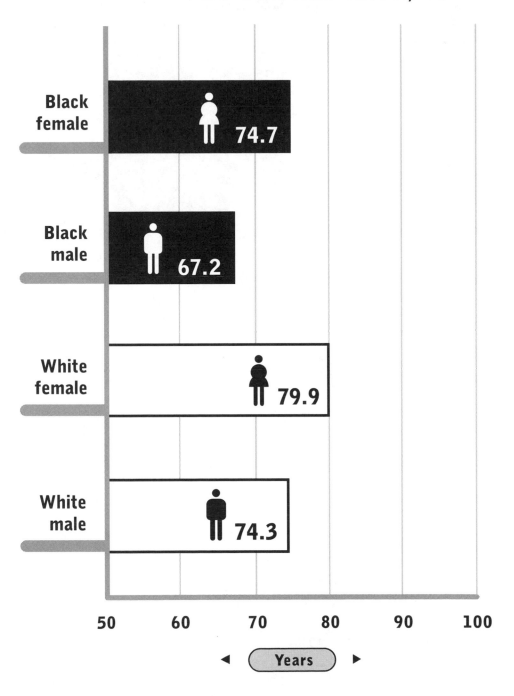

LIFE EXPECTANCY
BY SEX AND RACE, 1999

Black female — 74.7

Black male — 67.2

White female — 79.9

White male — 74.3

50 60 70 80 90 100

◄ Years ►

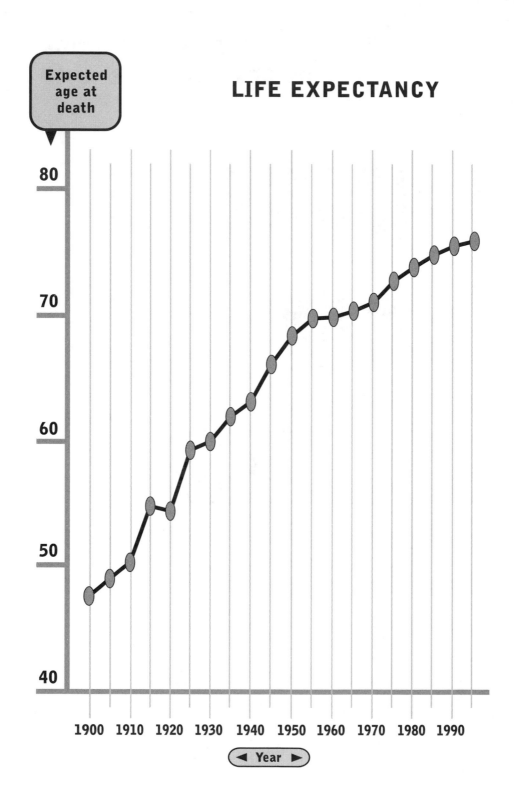

LIFE EXPECTANCY

Expected age at death

Medicine's Charge

Medicine has advanced farther in the past two hundred years than in the rest of history combined. Many diseases that were often fatal only fifty years ago have been nearly eradicated or are readily treated. Seldom do Americans now die of polio or malaria, let alone dysentery or typhoid.

The nineteenth-century discovery that many diseases are caused by infectious germs proved seminal, leading to the adoption of hygienic standards in hospitals, the development of vaccinations, and a better understanding of how to prevent diseases like cholera from spreading and becoming epidemic. And with the introduction of penicillin in 1941, a new age of antibiotic "wonder drugs" was initiated.

Medicine's advance, however, remains far from complete. Although some infectious diseases, such as smallpox, have been eliminated entirely, many bacterial killers once thought vanquished, most notably staph and tuberculosis, have become resistent to antibiotic treatments. Doctors still lack any surefire means of terminating viruses like herpes, influenza, and the common cold after infection has set in. And after the explosion of HIV in the early 1980s, public health officials are wary that under the right conditions new viral diseases—encephalitis, Ebola, dengue fever—could quickly spread throughout the United States.

Perhaps, though, the most radical revolution in medical treatment still awaits us. The 1953 discovery of DNA's double-helix structure has been followed by attempts—many successful—to discover the genetic basis of inherited conditions and to discover why some people are more susceptible to particular diseases and ailments. Not only has this aided in the development of conventional pharmaceuticals, but as scientists interpret the human genome, it raises the possibility that gene therapy may render many traditional cures obsolete.

Infant Mortality: Wealth Brings Health

Human babies enter the world with soft skulls, weak immune systems, and little motor control. Without advanced medical knowledge, their survival is at risk. In the United States of 1915, almost 100 infants out of every 1,000 died before their first birthday. That the infant mortality rate had dropped to 7.3 deaths per 1,000 by 1997 reflects major advances in medicine.

But these gains have not been distributed uniformly. At 14.2 deaths per 1,000, African American infants are 2.4 times more likely to die than white infants, whose mortality rate is 6 per 1,000. Infant mortality is also high among Native Americans, at 10 per 1,000. On the other hand, among Chinese Americans the rate is only slightly more than 3 per 1,000.

Education, though, may be the key to protecting infant health. A baby born to a mother with at least some college education is 62 percent more likely to reach childhood than one born to a high-school dropout. The correlation between education and infant health may reflect both the direct effects of learning—educated women are more informed about the need for prenatal care—and the greater affluence, and hence improved health services, that accompanies higher education.

INFANT MORTALITY

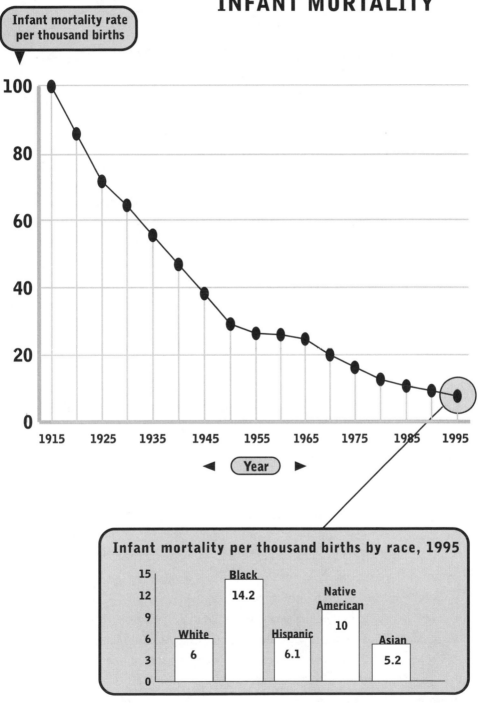

Infant mortality rate per thousand births

Year ◀ ▶

Infant mortality per thousand births by race, 1995

- White 6
- Black 14.2
- Hispanic 6.1
- Native American 10
- Asian 5.2

The Demography of Destiny: Genetic Diseases

By and large, cautious lifestyle choices and a bit of money for the doctor can keep a person healthy, but we are predisposed toward some ailments from birth. Such problems have long been cases of incurably bad luck, but as the mysteries of DNA are progressively unlocked, scientists are beginning to understand how we can defy fate.

A baby is born with a genetic inheritance from each of its parents. These genes serve as the blueprint for a baby's initial characteristics—physical and mental, good and bad, healthy and deadly. Usually, though, the deadly is avoided: most particularly dangerous genes are "recessive," which means that their place in the blueprint can be taken by healthy genes from the other parent. But if the same dangerous gene comes from both parents, the baby's health is at risk. The different risks for particular genetic diseases to which the different sexes and ethnic groups are subject are not consequences of social or economic injustice, but of this complex mechanism of human reproduction.

For instance, men are more susceptible than women to hemophilia, Fragile X syndrome, and one type of muscular dystrophy. This is because men have less distinct genetic material than women and receive some genes from only one parent. If one of these genes is dangerous, the baby will be negatively affected—even if the gene is recessive.

New genes—whether malignant or beneficial—originate in mutations, which are accidents that occur when a parent's genes are being copied for his or her child. That child, then, can pass the new gene on to his or her own children. Throughout history, persons have been most likely to have sex with members of their own "group," for reasons of both geography and prejudice.

GENETIC RISK OF SELECT DISEASES

Disease	Group most susceptible	Odds*
Tay-Sachs	Ashkenazi Jews	1 / 30
Sickle-cell anemia	African American	1 / 375
Fragile X Syndrome	Men	1 / 1,200
Hemophelia	Men	1 / 10,000
Ataxia-Telangiectasia	Ashkenazi Jews	1 / 300,000

* Chance of being a carrier

As a consequence, some genes are unusually common among particular groups. African Americans, for example, are unusually likely to carry the gene for sickle-cell anemia, which will dangerously deform the baby's blood cells if it is given a copy by both parents. Jews with ancestors from Eastern Europe are unusually likely to carry the genes for a variety of diseases, including Tay-Sachs, which destroys the nervous systems, and Ataxia-Telangiectasia, which severely damages both the nervous and immune systems. Cystic fibrosis, another genetic disease, primarily effects people with Northern European and British origins.

HOW AIDS IS TRANSMITTED

The chart shows relative prevalence of different means of HIV transmission. Data are based on AIDS cases as of December 1996.

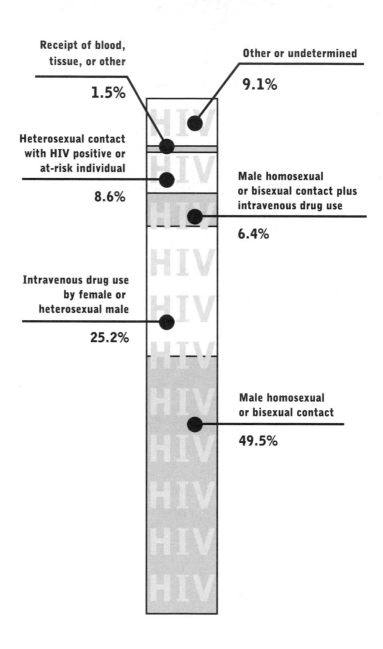

Receipt of blood, tissue, or other
1.5%

Other or undetermined
9.1%

Heterosexual contact with HIV positive or at-risk individual
8.6%

Male homosexual or bisexual contact plus intravenous drug use
6.4%

Intravenous drug use by female or heterosexual male
25.2%

Male homosexual or bisexual contact
49.5%

People with AIDS

After medicine took pride in its conquest—or at least containment—of the most deadly infectious diseases of the early twentieth century, the past decades have confronted it with a disease it has yet to defeat: AIDS. As of mid 1998, 665,357 cases of AIDS in the United States had been reported to the Centers for Disease Control and Prevention. Women make up only about 16 percent of all AIDS cases. Likewise, there has been much variation between ethnic communities: in 1997, 45 percent of all new AIDS cases were among African Americans, 33 percent were among whites, and 21 percent were among Latinos.

In the world as a whole, HIV—the virus that causes AIDS—is primarily acquired through heterosexual sex. In the United States, however, the situation is substantially different.

Two myths have plagued American beliefs about AIDS. The first, prevalent in the 1980s, was that AIDS was exclusively a disease of homosexual men—the "gay plague." Although this belief, of course, is false, it prevented federal outreach to people with AIDS throughout the 1980s. Tens of thousands of young gay men had died before Ronald Reagan first said the word "AIDS" in public in 1985. AIDS activists with their survival on the line—most of them gay men—struggled to make the epidemic a mainstream concern. In a way, they succeeded; by the 1990s, AIDS was accepted as a concern for all Americans, not just the gay population. At the same time, this shift of focus has sometimes drawn attention away from those most affected. While the media emphasizes the rising rates of infection among heterosexual men and women, the majority of recent HIV transmissions—about 52 percent—have been between gay and bisexual men. AIDS has been, and still is, primarily a young gay man's disease. And AIDS is the single leading cause of death among young African American men today.

Massive educational campaigns to encourage the use of condoms have been effective. Education and safe-sex practices have been lowering the rate of HIV infection in the United States for years. New AIDS cases have dropped since their 1993 peak of 103,533. Since then, the number of new cases has leveled off at approximately 40,000 per year. However, rates are rising again within some groups, most notably those who felt the epidemic first and hardest: young gay men.

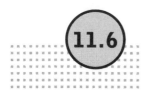

The Uninsured

The United States has some of the best doctors, hospitals, and medical technology in the world, but access to its quality care is far from universal: 43 million people, or 16 percent of the U.S. population, have no health insurance of any kind. In the 1990s, a hopeful national discussion began in Washington about insuring these uninsured, but consensus was elusive and the debate had fizzled out by the end of the decade. However, not all uninsured Americans are alike, and both opponents and advocates of health care reform have often glossed over the complexity of America's uninsured population.

For starters, there are severe regional differences in how many people are insured. Texas, for example, allows 25 percent of its residents to go uninsured—the highest proportion of any of the fifty states. And people of color are significantly less likely to own insurance. Over 35 percent of Latinos and 22 percent of African Americans have no health insurance, compared to 12 percent of the white population.

In the end, health insurance in America is an economic affair—a benefit earned by labor power or a purchasing decision made by those who can afford it. As income increases, so do the odds of being insured. Among those whose income is $75,000 a year or more, and hence could presumably afford insurance, 8 percent remain uninsured. Yet millions cannot afford coverage at all: 25 percent of those earning less than $25,000 have no insurance. And working Americans' chances of having insurance vary with the size of their employers. Those working for small businesses are much less likely to be covered than those employed by large corporations.

THE UNINSURED BY INCOME, 1998

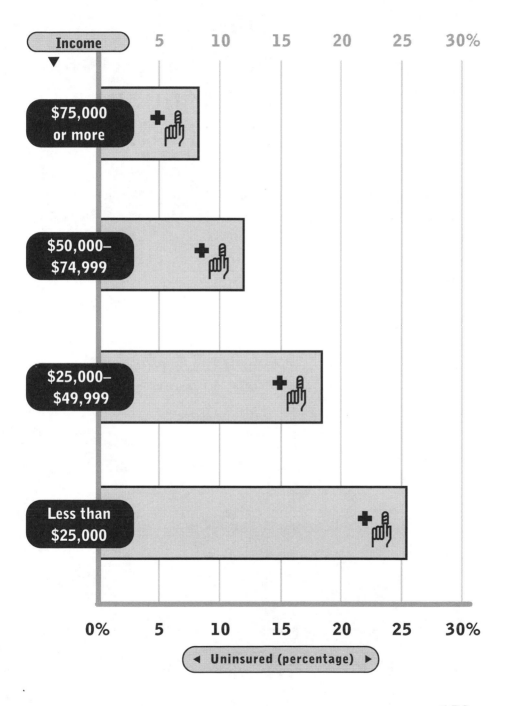

Income

$75,000 or more

$50,000– $74,999

$25,000– $49,999

Less than $25,000

◀ Uninsured (percentage) ▶

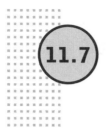

Smoking:
The Apolitical
Consequences
of Inhaling

The decision to start smoking is one of the riskiest lifestyle choices a person can make. In an age when one is bombarded by reports of the purported danger of everything from silicone to cell phones, cigarettes stand out for the overwhelming body of evidence demonstrating their dangers: lung cancer, mouth cancer, emphysema, heart disease, and so on. Indeed, ciga-

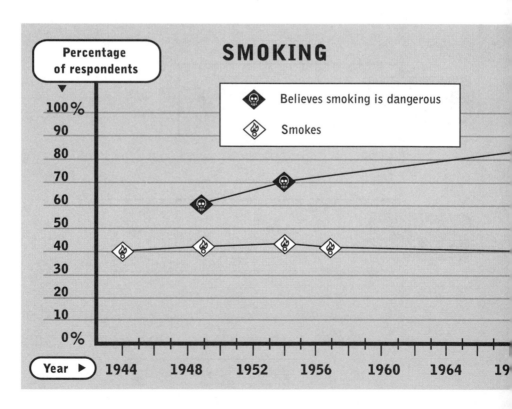

rettes contribute to 420,000 deaths each year. Despite the risks, about seven thousand teenagers per week began to smoke in 1998.

Today, 95 percent of Americans have been persuaded that smoking is harmful to their health and 76 percent of smokers say they want to quit. Indeed, the mounting knowledge of smoking's danger has been winnowing the ranks of smokers for decades: in 1954, 45 percent of adults smoked; in 1999, the proportion was down to 23 percent.

Over the past several decades, the percentage of people who believe that "cigarette smoking is harmful" has jumped to 95%, while the percentage of people who have "smoked any cigarettes in the past week" has fallen to 23%.

1972 1976 1980 1984 1988 1992 1996

DISABLED EARNINGS, 1997

Earnings are for individuals 21 to 64 years old.

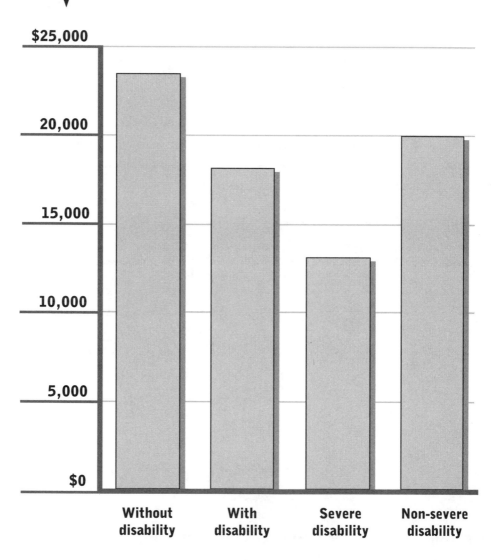

Median earnings (dollars)

$25,000

20,000

15,000

10,000

5,000

$0

Without disability | With disability | Severe disability | Non-severe disability

Disabled America

Historically the disabled have often failed to be recognized as a discrete subpopulation, viewed instead as isolated "cripples" or "invalids." For many, the only hint that "disabled" might be a social identity of its own has come from the blue icons in parking spaces and on restroom doors.

But the disabled population is far larger and far better organized than many Americans would guess. Depending on how "disability" is defined, as few as one in fifty, or as many as one out of every two Americans are disabled. The Census Bureau's definition yields a middle-range figure: approximately 35 million, or about one of every eight people in the United States. Although the wheelchair icon has come to symbolize the disabled population, it is hardly an accurate portrayal. While 24.5 percent of the U.S. population between forty-five and fifty-four years of age has a disability, only 0.4%, or 1 in 250 middle-aged Americans uses a wheelchair.

In 1990, partly as a result of pressure from the increasingly cohesive disabled community, Congress passed the Americans with Disabilities Act, securing a legal means of grievance against public inaccessibility and job discrimination. But even under the ADA, employment rates within the disabled community remain low. Disabled adults of working age (between twenty-one and sixty-five years) are 42.5 percent less likely to be employed than those without disabilities. And only two out of every nine wheelchair-bound persons of working age holds a job. In part, disabilities themselves keep the disabled out of the labor force—8.6 million working-age adults have disabilities severe enough to prevent work of any kind. But of the more than 20 million who are able to work, only 43.3 percent are employed. The stigma of disability and barriers to accessibility in workplaces lead to low rates of career advancement and job satisfaction among the working disabled. Indeed, the rate of discontent with one's workplace paces the severity of one's disability. The more severely disabled are more than twice as dissatisfied about their freedom and opportunities for advancement at work than those without disabilities and three times more likely to have serious worries about their job security.

Evading Death: New Threats, New Tactics

As the twentieth century's medical advances have routed some threats, others have become all the more salient. In the early 1900s, influenza, tuberculosis, and other infectious diseases were major killers. The 1918 influenza epidemic alone claimed 20 million lives. But, by 1997, pneumonia and influenza together were responsible for only around 86,000 deaths, dropping from the number one cause of death to number six.

Today, cancer and heart disease are far more threatening afflictions. Although the treatment and prevention of each improved substantially in the 1990s, they continue to claim more lives than any other causes of death. In 1997, cancer killed 539,577 people and heart disease killed 726,974 people in the United States.

TOP TEN CAUSES OF DEATH, THEN AND NOW

1900		1997
Pneumonia and flu	1	Heart Disease
Tuberculosis	2	Cancer
Diarrhea and intestinal ills	3	Stroke and brain lesions
Heart disease	4	Lung Disease
Stroke and brain lesions	5	Accidents
Kidney inflammation	6	Pneumonia and flu
Accidents	7	Diabetes
Cancer	8	Suicide
Senility	9	Kidney inflammation
Diphtheria	10	Liver disease

12

CRIMINALS

Violence and Confinement

Politicians and the mass media adore crime because crime frightens the public, hitting home like few other social issues. It is important to keep these fears in perspective—something demographic statistics can help us do. For instance, the U.S. murder rate, though higher than that of many industrialized countries, is not extraordinary and has declined significantly in recent years. Most crime rates are simply fluctuating; they forebode neither apocalypse nor utopia. Other trends, however, have had more consistent direction and less ambiguous consequence. The American rate of incarceration soared in the last decades of the twentieth century. Executions are mounting, the market for prison labor is booming, and millions of Americans have lost their right to vote due to felon disenfranchisement laws dating to the rollback of Reconstruction. Because these trends weigh disproportionately upon people of color, the American social contract may be called into question.

Guns and
the American Dream

Violence is at the heart of American mythology. We are all familiar with stories of the stalwart minutemen of 1776, of self-reliant musket-bearing pioneers, of cowboys with six-shooters, and of Prohibition-era gunfights between mobsters and G-men. As black militant H. Rap Brown once said, "Violence is as American as cherry pie."

Of course, this mythology is neither wholly true nor wholly false. On the one hand, during Revolutionary times, not even 10 percent of households owned working guns; even the militias were often poorly armed. On the other hand, the prevalence of guns increased dramatically with the advent of modern manufacturing methods and the Civil War. This prevalence shows few signs of change, in part because progun lobbies continue to push for a broad interpretation of the Constitution's Second Amendment: "A well regulated Militia being necessary to the security of a free State, the right of the people to keep and bear Arms, shall not be infringed."

But growing public outcry over shootings at schools, workplaces, and on the streets has forced a reevaluation of national priorities. The Brady Bill and similar laws have begun to mandate waiting periods and criminal background checks for gun buyers. And litigation brought by states against handgun manufacturers has placed the industry and its partisans on the political defensive.

A HISTORY OF GUNS IN AMERICA

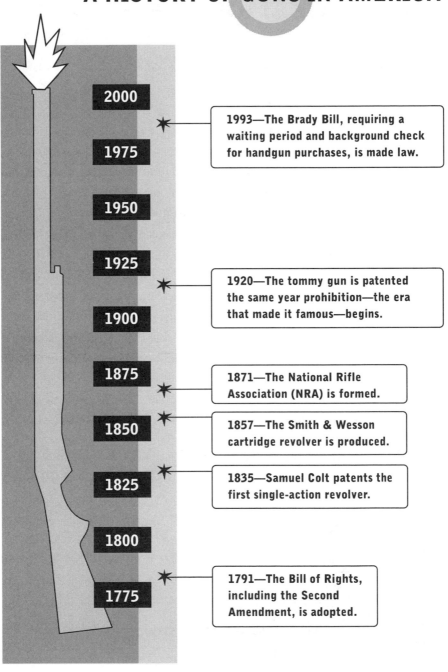

2000

1993—The Brady Bill, requiring a waiting period and background check for handgun purchases, is made law.

1975

1950

1925

1920—The tommy gun is patented the same year prohibition—the era that made it famous—begins.

1900

1875

1871—The National Rifle Association (NRA) is formed.

1850

1857—The Smith & Wesson cartridge revolver is produced.

1825

1835—Samuel Colt patents the first single-action revolver.

1800

1775

1791—The Bill of Rights, including the Second Amendment, is adopted.

America the Violent?

American violence is more than anecdotal. In 1998 the United States' murder rate was 1.5 times higher than Italy's, more than 4 times Canada's, and over 6 times Japan's.

On the other hand, people are more often scared by images in the media than by personal experience. The entertainment industry's exaggerated violence and the sensationalization of a few serial murderers obscure the fact that only about one out of eleven thousand people are killed each year, and in most areas the numbers are far better. In a very real sense, the United States remains a lawful country. Russia has a murder rate 2.6 times higher; Colombia's is nearly 9 times the U.S. rate. In most of the United States we are fairly safe.

Of course, it is easy to understand why the United States is experiencing less mortal violence than countries in the midst of civil war, like Colombia, or social upheaval, like Russia and Zimbabwe. But to explain why its murder rate is so high in comparison to countries in similar situations, one must look to underlying social problems, a culture that glamorizes violence, and laws that make it unusually easy to obtain a gun.

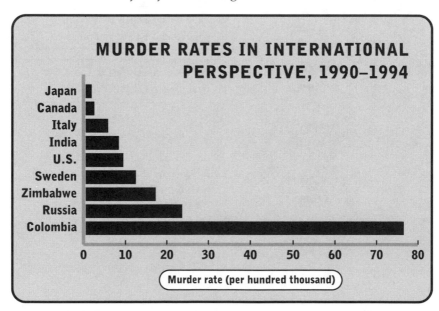

MURDER RATES IN INTERNATIONAL PERSPECTIVE, 1990–1994

Murder rate (per hundred thousand)

Murder Rates Vary by Region

Homicide rates vary greatly within the United States. Much of this variation is between some particularly violent cities and the generally more peaceful rural and suburban areas. Even when this difference is taken into account, some regions of the country clearly show a greater tendency toward violence than others. The South, in particular, has gained a reputation for mortal violence—a reputation that is merited by the statistics.

Policy makers and scholars advance a number of explanations for the regional violence gap. The most important of these are: high temperatures (and hence hot tempers), the sordid legacy of slavery, high poverty, and a "culture of honor." While each of these factors doubtless plays a role, cultural psychologists Richard Nisbett and Dov Cohen argue that it is the "necessity for men to appear strong and unwilling to tolerate an insult" that is the key to the South's distinctive pattern of violence.

MURDER RATES BY STATE, 1998

On a state-by-state basis, murder rates are highest in the Deep South.

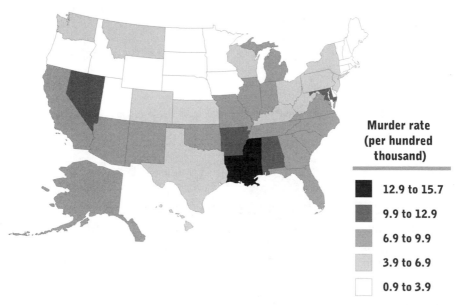

Murder rate (per hundred thousand)

- 12.9 to 15.7
- 9.9 to 12.9
- 6.9 to 9.9
- 3.9 to 6.9
- 0.9 to 3.9

But Things Aren't Getting Worse

Confusion regarding the prevalence of crime is widespread. While the rates of both violent and property crime fell throughout the 1990s, year after year most of the population believed that crime was on the rise (1999 was the only exception). Sensational news coverage played its part, but even the most stolidly statistical reportage is often deceptive. The "crime rate," or crime index, is produced by counting up a variety of crimes ranging from murder to larceny. A sudden jump in lawn-ornament theft raises the rate every bit as much as a commensurate jump in murders.

It is more meaningful to look at the rates of more specific crimes, but even then there is confusion. The government estimates crime rates using two different methods, one based on police records, the other on a national survey asking people whether they have been victim to various crimes. While each estimate has it own strengths and shortcomings, that produced using

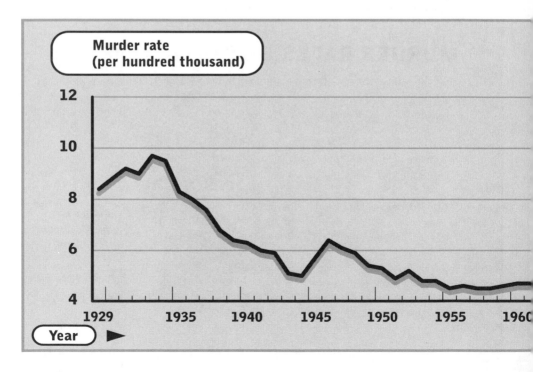

the survey probably more accurately reflects changes in the frequency of criminal acts. The use of police records to estimate such rates can have problematic, even paradoxical, consequences. For instance, communities faced with unacceptable levels of crime often elect to enlarge their police forces, tighten enforcement policies, or criminalize previously legal activities. If these measures are successful, they will—at least temporarily—increase the number of crimes police find out about. If this increase is then interpreted as a rise in crime, what began as citizens' concern for their safety can become panic at crime spinning out of control. And the actual rate of crime need not change at all.

In the end, it seems that public perceptions of crime are shaped more by the actions of journalists and the complexities of crime statistics than by the social change.

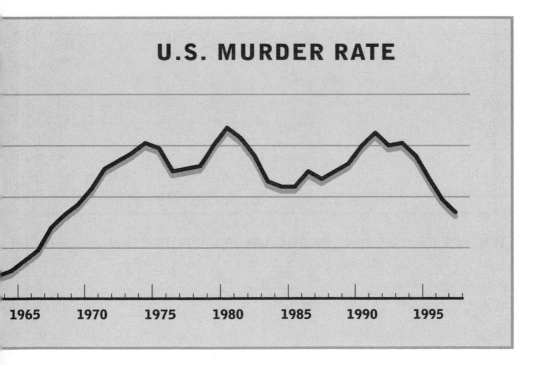

U.S. MURDER RATE

1965   1970   1975   1980   1985   1990   1995

EXECUTIONS

The Supreme Court's 1972 decision that the application of the death penalty had been "harsh, freakish, and arbitrary" brought executions to a halt. But new state laws regulating the death penalty were approved in 1976; executions recommenced soon thereafter.

Number of executions

200

150

100

50

0

1930 1935 1940 1945 1950 1955 1960 1965 1970 1975 1980 1985 1990 1995

◄ Year ►

12.5

An Eye
for an Eye:
Capital
Punishment
in America

America's response to societal violence has often been state violence. The United States has a long tradition of executing criminals.

Relying on the simplicity of the Old Testament aphorism "an eye for an eye," many Americans fail to realize how anomalous our use of capital punishment is. Most European countries phased it out in the early nineteenth century. Now they commonly view it as a barbarism; in fact, Turkey's application for European Union candidacy was nearly sunk by its continued use of the death penalty.

As the number of known innocents sentenced to death has risen, so has the outcry. One study found that 68 percent of death sentences are reversed on appeal. Of those whose sentences were reversed, most were found guilty on lesser charges, but 7 percent were actually found not guilty. In a number of cases, death-row inmates have been altogether exonerated—sometimes only shortly before their scheduled executions.

World opinion aside, however, America keeps on executing. Since capital punishment returned in 1977 after a brief hiatus due to a Supreme Court ruling, nearly seven hundred people have been put to death by the American justice system.

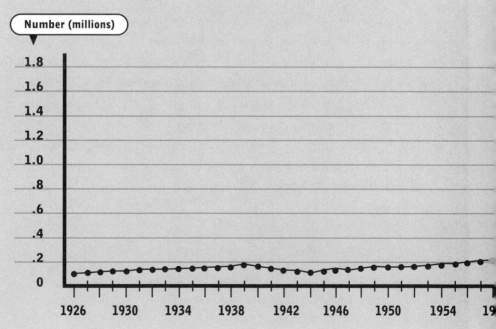

Number (millions)

1.8
1.6
1.4
1.2
1.0
.8
.6
.4
.2
0

1926   1930   1934   1938   1942   1946   1950   1954   19

12.6

The Prison Boom

While the murder rate has held fairly steady, incarceration rates in the United States have skyrocketed. In 1980, there were 501,886 people held in jail or prison; by 1996 that figure had risen to 1,637,928. Only Russia has a higher rate of incarceration than the United States.

This explosion in the prison population has been very expensive. The justice system cost a total of $112 billion in 1995, $430 for each American. In the same year, this vast system employed nearly 2 million people.

Neither an increase in murder nor an increase in other violence can be used to explain prison population growth. One instead needs to look toward increasingly stringent provisions, such as California's "three strikes" law, and mandatory minimum sentences for drug-related crimes.

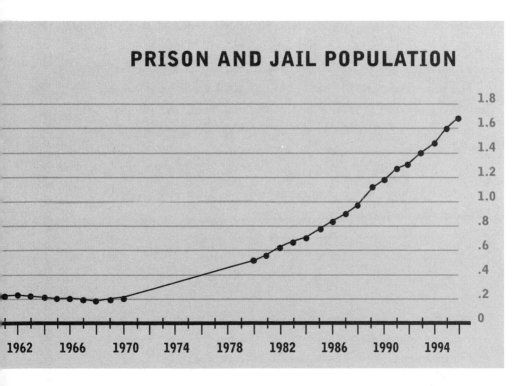

PRISON AND JAIL POPULATION

Punishment:
Life Without the Vote

While the United States has been broadly democratic since its inception, the right to vote has been at various times withheld from women, the land-less, African Americans, and Native Americans. In today's America, other than non-citizens, the only adults barred from the ballot box are many felons and ex-felons. All but two states—Maine and Vermont—disenfranchise at least those in prison. Many states prohibit even ex-felons from voting.

These felon disenfranchisement laws disproportionately affect people of color. According to the best available estimates, fully 1.3 million of the 4.2 million disenfranchised felons and ex-felons are black. In New Mexico, nearly 25 percent of black people have been disenfranchised. In Iowa, the number is 23 percent and in Mississippi, it's 10 percent. And not only do these laws have inequitable results, they were often enacted for just that rea-son. When white Southerners began to attack the gains of Reconstruction in the late nineteeneth century, they often targeted felon disenfranchisement laws at crimes black people disproportionately committed, while allowing people who had committed other crimes to vote. This resulted in such absurdities as a South Carolina law that barred thieves but not murderers.

The razor-thin margin of victory in the 2000 presidential contest drew further attention to the consequences of felon disenfranchisement. While those who are disenfranchised make up only a small proportion of the voting-aged population—about 2 percent—they are predominantly Democratic and could well have swung the election. If imprisonment had been as wide-spread as it is now, two sociologists have predicted that Richard Nixon could have defeated John F. Kennedy in 1960.

But even Democratic politicians are often loath to touch the issue, for fear of appearing "soft on crime." So people who have had their right to vote taken away have been turning to the courts. Not all legal scholars agree, but many find the state laws in violation of the Voting Rights Act. Civil rights advocates also are angry. After all, the struggle for the vote was a cornerstone of the civil rights movement; rather than moving forward, it appears to some that as incarceration rates soar, America is regressing.

CIVIC CONFINEMENT, 1998

In some states, felon disenfranchisement provisions prevent large portions of the population—especially African American men—from voting.

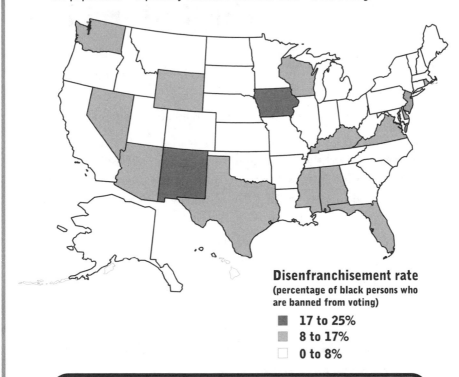

Disenfranchisement rate
(percentage of black persons who are banned from voting)

■ 17 to 25%
■ 8 to 17%
□ 0 to 8%

WHO ARE THE DISENFRANCHISED?

Most people who have lost the vote under felon disenfranchisement laws are not in prison. In fact, roughly one third are no longer in the correctional system at all.

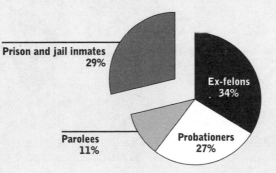

Prison and jail inmates
29%

Ex-felons
34%

Parolees
11%

Probationers
27%

12.8

Justice and the Color Line

Many believe that capital punishment and long prison sentences make everyone safer. But the hope for safety may have its cost; evidence shows that the American criminal justice system perpetuates traditional patterns of racial disparity.

Only 13 percent of the U.S. population is African American. But 38 percent of prisoners are African American, as are 41 percent of those on death row. This has led some to say that "legal lynching" has now taken the place of the lynchings of the old South.

The effects of this racial disparity are even more troubling due to the practices of accompanying prison terms with forced labor and lifetime disenfranchisement.

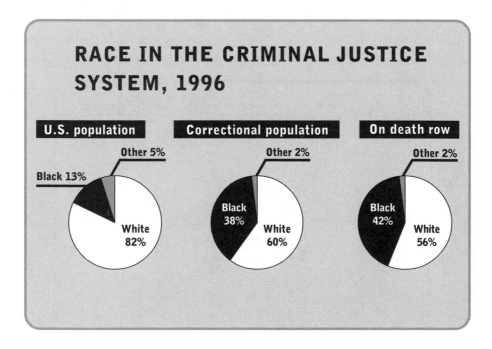

RACE IN THE CRIMINAL JUSTICE SYSTEM, 1996

U.S. population
Other 5%
Black 13%
White 82%

Correctional population
Other 2%
Black 38%
White 60%

On death row
Other 2%
Black 42%
White 56%

Prisons as Factories

Although chain gangs have been reintroduced in only a few states, prison labor has risen substantially over the last few decades. The number of prison laborers in the United States rose 358 percent from 1980 to include about seventy thousand prisoners in 1994. While most of these work for the public sector, a growing number of private companies hire convicts.

With wages averaging only 87¢ per hour and prisoners prohibited from organizing, prison labor is often found to be highly exploitative. Some prisoners have compared it to slavery. The employment of persons exempt from minimum-wage laws and without recourse to many of the rights of free workers, has angered labor unions. When Oregon passed a business-backed law mandating that all prisoners work, thousands of nonprison workers lost their jobs; it can be difficult to compete with workers paid so little.

PRISONS AS FACTORIES, 1992

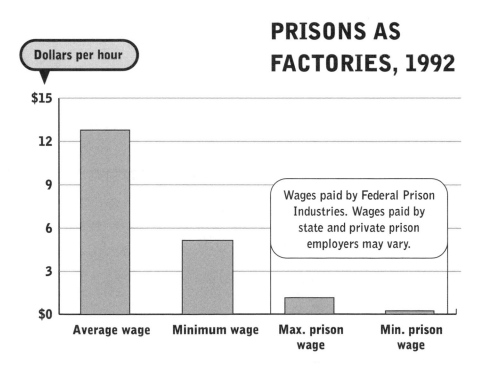

Dollars per hour

Wages paid by Federal Prison Industries. Wages paid by state and private prison employers may vary.

$15
12
9
6
3
$0

Average wage   Minimum wage   Max. prison wage   Min. prison wage

RAPE VICTIMIZATION

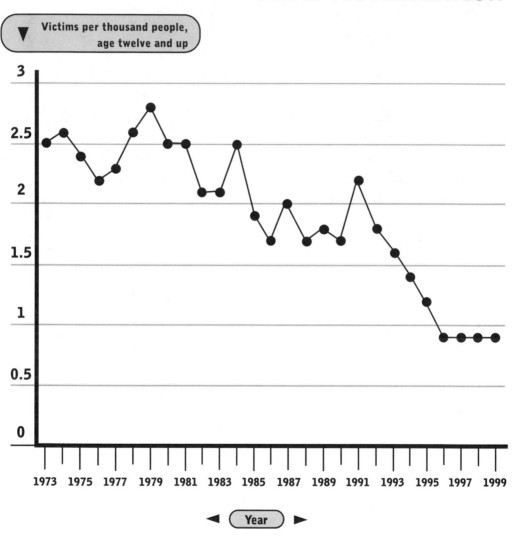

Victims per thousand people, age twelve and up

▼

3
2.5
2
1.5
1
0.5
0

1973 1975 1977 1979 1981 1983 1985 1987 1989 1991 1993 1995 1997 1999

◄ Year ►

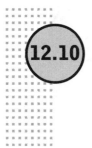

12.10

Violence
Against
Women

Violence against women contributes to a culture of fear that may persuade many women not to travel alone or late at night, not to dress in any way that might be deemed risqué, and even to be less assertive and independent.

There are many crimes—domestic violence, rape, sexual assault—for which the overwhelming majority of the victims are women. In 1996, 307,000 women—more than one woman every two minutes—were victims of rape. About half of rape victims are under eighteen and three quarters require medical care after the attack. And violence against women is rarely anonymous; more than half of American women who are murdered or raped know their assailant personally.

Fear of reprisal by the assailant, distrust in the effectiveness of law enforcement, or belief that the crime is a private matter prevent about 70 percent of rapes and sexual assaults from being reported to law enforcement officials.

The Violence of Hate

Hate crimes perennially belie America's much touted tolerance. Differences of religion, sexual orientation, ethnicity, and disability motivate murders, threatening graffiti, and church burnings. Nearly two thirds of hate crimes are racist. Indeed, over four thousand racist hate crimes were reported in 1998, and the Southern Poverty Law Center is aware of over five hundred hate groups active in the United States. Many states, however, do not have specific legislation to address such incidents. For instance, as of 2000, only twenty-one states and the District of Columbia had sentencing laws that recognized antigay hate crimes.

HATE CRIME MOTIVATIONS, 1996

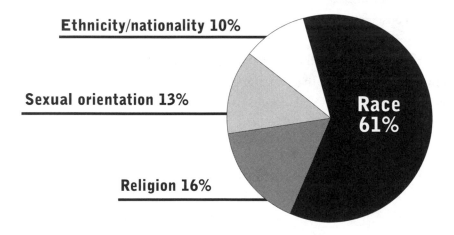

Ethnicity/nationality 10%

Sexual orientation 13%

Religion 16%

Race 61%

VOTERS

The Demography of Democracy

It is a commonplace of punditry to complain about America's general lack of political participation. Why so little participation, even when races for office seem close and most agree that their outcomes are important? A look at the statistics of American democracy can offer a few answers. Demographic data can tell us who participates and who does not, allowing us to speculate about causes and solutions. But these same data guide politicians in precisely targeting messages at narrow demographics—different issues for different people in different places. The aim is to get out the friendly vote, keep out the hostile vote, and leave the apathetic alone. Further, polling and demographic analyses require the technical expertise of highly paid consultants, often leaving grassroots support neglected. Now money seems to matter more than people. Rather than rallying the troops, politicians spend much of their time at thousand-dollar-a-plate dinners drumming up money for consultants, mailing lists, and television advertisements. The people behind the expensive plates are paying for a reason: access. They want their high-priority issues to be part of the politician's agenda. Meanwhile, the poor and much of the middle class grow cynical and disaffected. Unable to finance their own campaigns, they find politicians pushing agendas that ignore their priorities and mock their worldviews. With no politician of their own, they often stay home on Election Day.

The Making of the American Electorate

The United States has been a leader in democracy since its founding. But full political citizenship has always been denied to some of its residents, notably women, African Americans, and new immigrants.

Women launched the struggle for the ballot at the Seneca Falls Convention in 1848. But it was the First World War that laid the groundwork for the victory of the suffrage movement. Industrial work on the home front made women more visible participants in the nation's business. This change of status, together with high-profile activism, led to the national enfranchisement of women in 1920.

For African Americans, the path to the vote was more tortuous. In 1863, the Union issued the Emancipation Proclamation, and almost 180,000 of the newly freed joined the military to help win the war for the Union. In 1870, black male enfranchisement followed. But over the next four decades, state voting laws were enacted that effectively nullified African American voting rights in the South. The war that brought women's suffrage raised similar hopes among African Americans, but these hopes were left unfulfilled. Likewise, the Second World War inspired a campaign for victory against racism at home as well as abroad. This, too, was unsuccessful. It took the mass mobilization of the civil rights movement to reestablish Southern black voting rights in 1965.

Today, the right to vote among citizens of age eighteen and older is nearly universal; the remaining exception is that some states restrict the voting of felons.

A HISTORY OF THE RIGHT TO VOTE

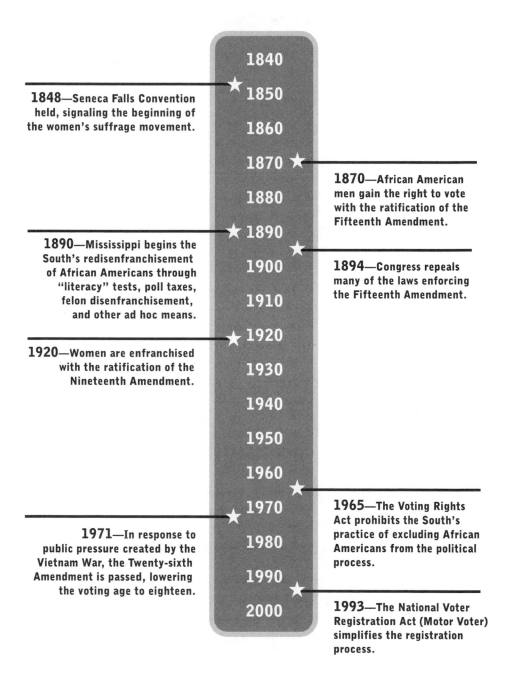

1840

1848—Seneca Falls Convention held, signaling the beginning of the women's suffrage movement.

1850

1860

1870

1870—African American men gain the right to vote with the ratification of the Fifteenth Amendment.

1880

1890

1890—Mississippi begins the South's redisenfranchisement of African Americans through "literacy" tests, poll taxes, felon disenfranchisement, and other ad hoc means.

1900

1894—Congress repeals many of the laws enforcing the Fifteenth Amendment.

1910

1920

1920—Women are enfranchised with the ratification of the Nineteenth Amendment.

1930

1940

1950

1960

1970

1965—The Voting Rights Act prohibits the South's practice of excluding African Americans from the political process.

1971—In response to public pressure created by the Vietnam War, the Twenty-sixth Amendment is passed, lowering the voting age to eighteen.

1980

1990

2000

1993—The National Voter Registration Act (Motor Voter) simplifies the registration process.

THE DEMOCRATS, 1996

A profile of those who identify themselves as Democrats

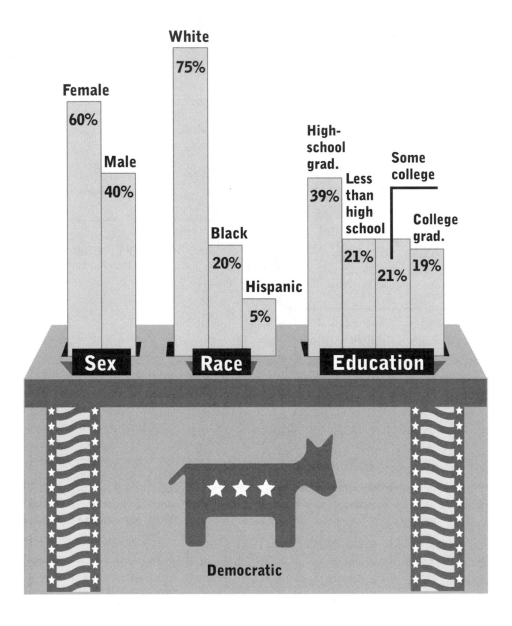

Who Are the Democrats?

For several decades, the Democratic Party has struggled to develop strong relations with the business community without alienating its key constituencies among workers and the poor. And although registered Democrats outnumber Republicans, the party has often had a difficult time turning its supporters out at the polls. Some, dubbed New Democrats, are positive toward business and supportive of cutbacks to the limited U.S. welfare state. Others wish the party to be a stalwart defender of the working class and government assistance to the poor.

When the Pew Research Center for the People and the Press conducted an in-depth study of the electorate in 1999, it found that Democrats fall into four basic "types": New Democrats, Liberal Democrats, Socially Conservative Democrats, and the Partisan Poor. All but the first group strongly believe that corporations make too much profit.

But the alliances are more complicated on social issues. For instance, while 88 percent of Liberals and 68 percent of New Democrats believe that gayness should be accepted by society, the highly religious Partisan Poor and Socially Conservative Democrats disagree (only 41 percent and 39 percent said yes, respectively). But, on the other hand, Liberals and the Partisan Poor are somewhat more tightly aligned on racial issues.

People of color make up one-quarter of the Democratic base, making the party far more diverse than the Republicans. However, because the votes of minorities are usually taken for granted by the Democrats, the party has been able to steer clear of explicitly racial issues that might risk alienating the white centrist population.

THE REPUBLICANS, 1996

A profile of those who
identify themselves as Republicans

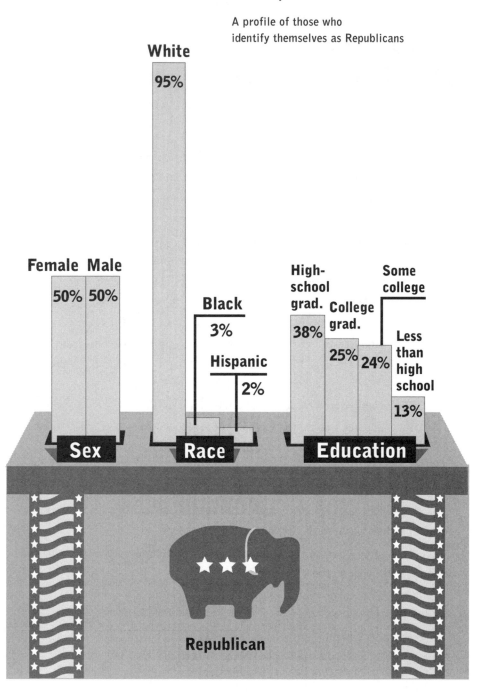

Who Are the Republicans?

The Republican Party has struggled even more than the Democrats to find positions acceptable to each of its core groups. For the GOP, the two key constituencies are the economically conservative business community and the socially conservative Christian Right. Neither group can be ignored without seriously compromising the party's strength. Indulging the wealthy, however, risks the support of poorer members brought into the fold by social fears, while moralistic rhetoric risks estranging all but a narrow group of supporters. In major campaigns, then, the party's strategy often becomes a rapid yet deliberate run from the political center to the right and back again.

The Pew typology divides the party's supporters into three groups: Staunch Conservatives, Populist Republicans, and Moderate Republicans. The older and more affluent Staunch Conservatives are true believers: they are skeptical of business regulation, unsympathetic toward the poor, promilitary, and hostile toward most social movements of the last several decades. On the other hand, the Populists are very socially conservative but uneasy with a probusiness ethic: 76 percent believe that books containing "dangerous ideas" should be banned from public school libraries while 75 percent believe that corporations make too much profit. The Moderates recall an older meaning of conservatism: satisfied with the status quo, they are proestablishment and relatively lacking in the cynicism that typifies the rest of the party.

Although Republican economic policies have come under much criticism, the party's deepest problem at the ballot box might be a perception of racial intolerance. The New Right's propensity to be callous toward minorities was highlighted when Ronald Reagan launched his 1980 campaign by proclaiming his support for "states' rights" in Philadelphia, Mississippi, the site of the infamous 1963 murder of Medgar Evers, a black civil rights worker. But as the U.S. population grows increasingly diverse, the party's dearth of nonwhite support may damage its electoral chances. To reverse this trend, Republican leaders have made a determined effort to reach out to the booming Latino population.

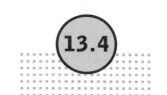

Who Remains Independent?

Independent voters share little but their disaffection. In one key group of independents, we find young and newly affluent beneficiaries of the "information economy"—the economic order suits them fine, but their enthusiasm does not extend to the political establishment. Too culturally tolerant for the GOP, their high incomes dissuade them from traditional Democratic policies. Undereducated blue-collar workers comprise a second key group of independents. Left behind by prosperity yet culturally conservative, they are deeply cynical about the government.

Although campaigns often find independents too alienated to be dependable voters, independents gain clout as "swing voters" who can be decisive at the polls precisely because they lack long-standing party loyalty. In 1992 and 1996, suburban "soccer moms" became key targets of each campaign, helping Bill Clinton to victory. By 2000, campaigns' approach to independents had spread to encompass such broad groups as Arab Americans and middle-income Latinos.

Many independents, though, identify strongest with an escape from the two-party system, voting for Reform, Green, Libertarian, or nonaligned candidates. Disgusted by Republicans and Democrats alike, many wish that a third party would rise to national prominence. Indeed, a majority of Americans—54 percent—say that they would like to have a third major party. The American electoral process, however, has preserved the two-party system with considerable success. Third-party candidates, whether driven by the enduring hopes of a few passionate activists or the personas of a few wealthy individuals, almost always fail to garner a substantial percentage of the vote.

THE INDEPENDENTS, 1996

A profile of those who consider themselves "independent"

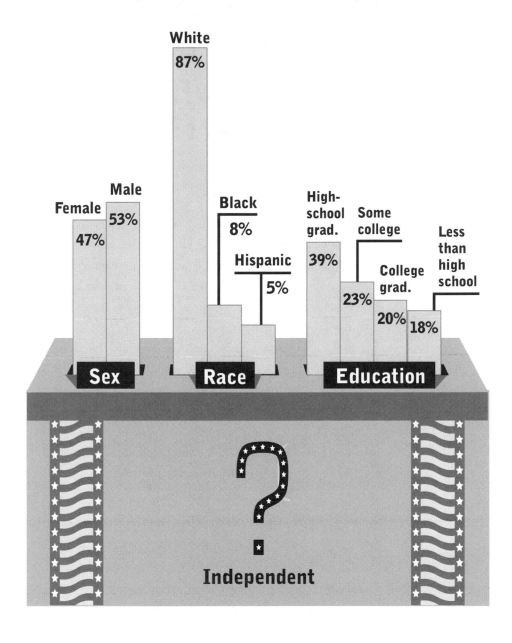

Female 47%   Male 53%

Sex

White 87%

Black 8%

Hispanic 5%

Race

High-school grad. 39%

Some college

College grad. 23%

20% 18%

Less than high school

Education

? · Independent

Are We Growing Apart?

America is getting older and the political implications of its aging may be profound; the material interests of the old are often at odds with those of the young. Although Americans broadly support the idea of Social Security, many turn against it when they see the drop in their paycheck as their earnings go to retirees. While parents want good schools for their children, grandparents may prove more concerned with Medicare.

Perhaps the central question is whether intergenerational bonds will prove strong enough to hold together our deeply individualistic society. But the question is complicated by the increasing diversity of the population. Predominantly white retirees will be called upon to help pay for the schooling of Latino and black children. And those children's parents will be providing for the well-being of the retirees. This interdependence may pull generations closer together, or divergent priorities may pull them apart.

PROPORTION VOTING BY AGE, 1996

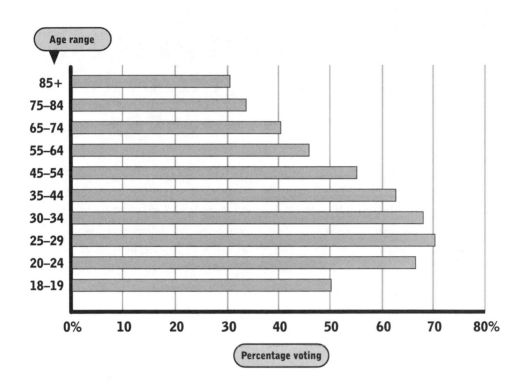

Age range

Percentage voting

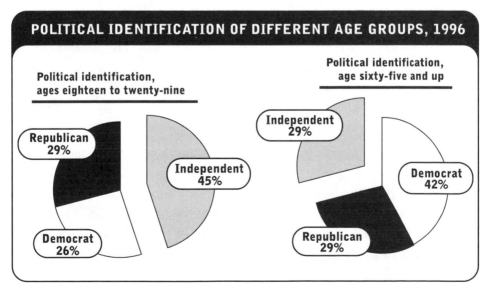

POLITICAL IDENTIFICATION OF DIFFERENT AGE GROUPS, 1996

Political identification,
ages eighteen to twenty-nine

Republican
29%

Independent
45%

Democrat
26%

Political identification,
age sixty-five and up

Independent
29%

Democrat
42%

Republican
29%

13.6

90210 and the Buying of the Presidency

Political campaigns are fueled by money—money for television advertisements and mass mailings, media consultants and pollsters, campaign managers and travel staff. It has become nearly impossible for a candidate to be elected to national office without a multimillion dollar "war chest." A Public Campaign study of the Federal Election Commission records from the early portion of the 2000 presidential race found that the bulk of political donations come from a small number of wealthy neighborhoods. Southern California offers an indicative example of the imbalance in contributions: while Beverly Hills had donated over $3 million, Watts provided only $2,750.

The top one hundred contributing neighborhoods (determined by zip codes) gave nearly one quarter of total political contributions. Areas where about 1 percent of the population live provide 23 percent of the campaign funds for the leading presidential candidates. The structure of American political finance is glaringly top-heavy.

Campaigns' dependency on fund-raising further aggravates the stratification of American politics. If they are to compete, candidates are compelled to spend much of their limited time at fund-raising receptions and dinners. As they become intimate with the concerns of the donating elite, the wishes of the rest of the population are left to be represented only by the impersonal polling statistic.

Not coincidentally, the views of the wealthy are closely bound to the interests of business and finance. Amplified by money, their voices are heard above the crowd of activists. Many voters are led to see the captains of industry as cocaptains of state; indeed, the data show that businesses contribute over nine times more to candidates and parties than labor unions do.

BUYING ACCESS, 2000

Politicians are much more dependent on some neighborhoods
than others.

Beverly Hills, 90210

Political donations	$3,022,583
White	91%
Black	2%
Hispanic (of any race)	6%
Poverty rate (for persons)	6%
Median value of owner-occupied houses	$500,000+ (top-coded)*

Watts, 90059

Political donations	$2,750
White	9%
Black	63%
Hispanic (of any race)	37%
Poverty rate (for persons)	39%
Median value of owner-occupied houses	$94,100

*NOTE: For privacy reasons the Census Bureau did not report exact values higher than $500,000.

There is a viable alternative, though perhaps not a better option: in the wake of billionaire Ross Perot's independent bid for the presidency in 1992 and 1996, the extraordinarily rich have often funded their own campaigns, escaping federal spending regulations. Indeed, the Congress elected in 2000 included a record number of multimillionaires, several of whom unseated incumbents through personally financed media blitzes.

VOTER TURNOUT

Turnout for presidential elections—the percentage
of the voting-age population who exercise their
vote has never been slimmer.

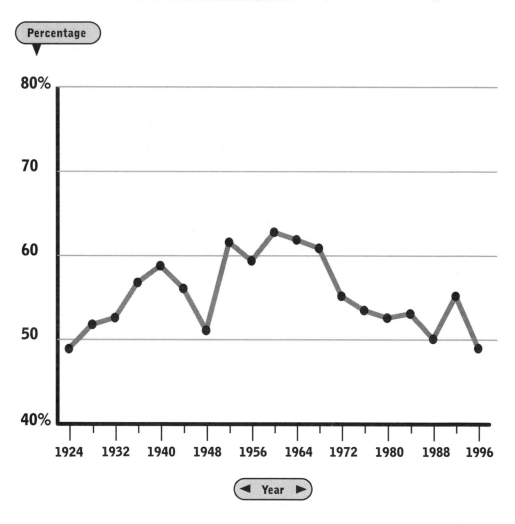

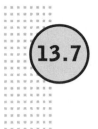

13.7

Voter
Apathy

It sometimes seems that Americans just do not care. Voter turnout statistics validate this widespread belief: in the 1996 presidential election only 66 percent of those registered to vote did so. Even in the perilously close presidential race of 2000, turnout remained well below what it had been as recently as 1992.

Why do so many people choose not to vote? The reason revolves around a growing alienation from politics, politicians, and the electoral process. Politicians are seen as either cynical and self-interested or hopelessly beholden to special-interest lobbyists. When nobody seems to represent them, little can motivate an American to vote, let alone to volunteer for a campaign or to run for office.

How did America become so disaffected? The shifting nature of political campaigns offers one answer. Once, for a candidate to succeed, she had to successfully balance grassroots organization, public rallying, and active local participation in her constituents' lives. Today, however, campaigns are aloof and impersonal; when a campaign survives, it lives off mass mailing, six-second sound bites, and "instant organizations" paid to win elections and then fold up shop. All of this places a premium on technology and professional expertise, relegating voters and volunteers to the sidelines.

Class Participation: Grade: F

There is a clear and well-defined correlation between income and political participation. Not only are those with higher incomes more likely to vote, but they are also more likely to volunteer for electoral and activist campaigns. The poor are often left behind as political targets rather than political actors.

A lack of political participation by the poor can quickly create a vicious circle. A political agenda set by the wealthy often alienates the poor. But, by removing themselves from the political decision-making process, they allow the major parties to continue to disregard their policy priorities.

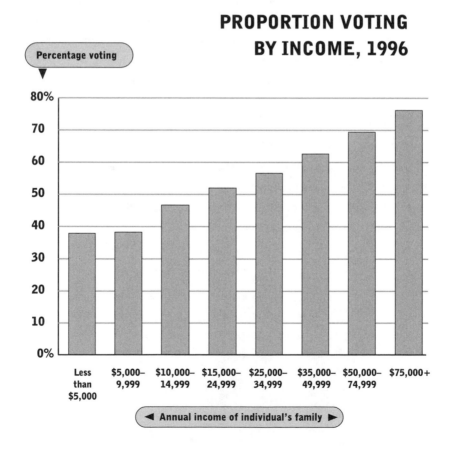

PROPORTION VOTING BY INCOME, 1996

SOURCES

1. Generations

1.1 Population Growth
U.S. Census Bureau.
1.2 The Architecture of Population
1990 U.S. Census 5% Public Use Microdata Set (PUMS).
1.3 The Greatest Generation
1990 U.S. Census 5% PUMS; General Social Survey (GSS).
1.4 The Lucky Generation
U.S. Census Bureau; GSS; Leon F. Bouvier and Carol J. De Vita, "The Baby Boom: Entering Midlife," *Population Bulletin* (1991); William H. Frey, "America's Demography in the New Century," *Urban Land* (January 2000).
1.5 The Baby Boom's Demography
U.S. Census Bureau; GSS; Bouvier and De Vita, "The Baby Boom;" Frey, "America's Demography in the New Century."
1.6 Generation X
GSS; U.S. Census Bureau.
1.7 Generation Y
U.S. Census Bureau; Ronald Inglehart, *Human Values and Beliefs: A Cross-Cultural Sourcebook: Political, Religious, Sexual, and Economic Norms in 43 Societies; Findings from the 1990–1993 World Value Survey* (Ann Arbor: Michigan, 1998); Nancy Shepherdson, "Life's a Beach 101," *American Demographics* (May 2000).

2. Sexes

2.1 Glass Ceilings, Sticky Floors, Pink Collars
U.S. Census Bureau, March 1998 Current Population Study, from National Committee on Pay Equity; U.S. Census Bureau, Statistical Brief, *Two Different Worlds: Men and Women from 9 to 5*.
2.2 Sex × Race
Teresa Amott and Julie Matthaei, *Race, Gender, and Work* (Boston, Mass.: South End Press, 1996); data from U.S. Census Bureau; National

Committee on Pay Equity.
2.3 Out of the Home
GSS; U.S. Census Bureau.
2.4 Women in Time
Kathleen C. Berkeley, *Attitudinal Feminism: The Women's Liberation Movement in America* (Westport, Conn.: Greenwood Press, 1999); Patricia Aburdene and John Naisbitt, *Megatrends for Women* (New York: Villard Books, 1992); Women's Research and Education Institute, ed. Cynthia B. Costello, Shari E. Miles, and Anne J. Stone, *The American Woman 1999–2000* (New York: W. W. Norton, 1998).
2.5 Feminist Values and the Fear of "Feminism"
GSS; Kathleen C. Berkeley, *Attitudinal Feminism: The Women's Liberation Movement in America* (Westport, Conn.: Greenwood Press, 1999).
2.6 Counting in the Closet
Annette Bennett, L. Singer, and David Deschamps, *Gay and Lesbian Statistics* (New York: The New Press, 1994); Amy J. Zuckerman and George F. Simons, *Sexual Orientation in the Workplace* (Santa Cruz, Calif.: International Partners Press, 1994); Kinsey Institute for Research in Sex, Gender, and Reproduction, "Prevalence of Homosexuality: Brief Summary of U.S. Studies" (1999); Tom Smith, "American Sexual Behavior" (1998).
2.7 Lavender Ghettos and the Rights Closet
Gallup, 2000; Bennett, Singer, and Deschamps, *Gay and Lesbian Statistics*; Zuckerman and Simons, *Sexual Orientation in the Workplace*.
2.8 From Mattachine to Stonewall to Queer
Bennett, Singer, and Deschamps, *Gay and Lesbian Statistics;* Zuckerman and Simons, *Sexual Orientation in the Workplace*.

3. Peoples

3.1 African Americans
1990 U.S. Census; census questionnaires and enumerator instructions; Michael Omi and Howard Winant, *Racial Formation in the United States* (New York: Routledge, 1994); Margo J. Anderson. *The American Census: A Social History* (New Haven, Conn.: Yale University Press, 1988); George P. Rawick, "From Sundown to Sunup: Slavery and the Making of the Black Community," in *Origins and Destinies: Immigration, Race, and Ethnicity in America*, ed. Silvia Pedraza and Rubén G. Rumbaut (Belmont, Calif.: Wadsworth, 1996).
3.2 A Revolution in White Attitudes
Howard Schuman and Charlotte Steeh, "The Complexity of Racial Attitudes in America," in *Origins*, above.
3.3 White People
U.S. Census Bureau; Hasia Diner, "Erin's Children in America: Three Centuries of Irish Immigration to the United States," in *Origins*, above; Richard D. Alba, "Italian Americans: A Century of Ethnic Change," in *Origins*, above.
3.4 Native Americans
1990 U.S. Census; Russell Thornton, *American Indian Holocaust and Survival: A Population History since 1492* (Norman: University of

Oklahoma Press, 1987); Russell Thornton, "North Americans and the Demography of Contact," in *Origins*, above; Stephen Cornell, "American Indians and Political Protest: The 'Red Power' Years," in *Origins*, above.

3.5 What Is "Hispanic"?
1990 Census 5% PUMS; Ricardo Romo, "Mexican Americans: Their Civic and Political Incorporation," in *Origins*, above; Sherri Grasmuck and Patricia Pessar, "Dominicans in the United States: First- and Second-Generation Settlement," in *Origins*, above; Anderson, *The American Census*.

3.6 Asian American Diversity
1990 Census 5% PUMS; Anderson, *The American Census*.

3.7 America's Developing Diversity
Ruth B. McKay and Manuel de la Puente, "Cognitive Testing of Racial and Ethnic Questions for the Current Population Survey Supplement," *Monthly Labor Review* (September 1996).

4. Immigrants

4.1 The History of Immigration
A. Dianne Schmidley and Campbell Gibson, *Profile of the Foreign-Born Population in the United States: 1997*, U.S. Census Bureau, Current Population Reports, series P3–195; *Legal Immigration, Fiscal Year 1998*, U.S. Department of Justice, Immigration and Naturalization Service, Office of Policy and Planning Annual Report (May 1999); Silvia Pedraza, "Origins and Destinies: Immigration, Race, and Ethnicity in American History," in *Origins and Destinies*, ed. Silvia Pedraza and Rubén G. Rumbaut (Belmont, Calif.: Wadsworth, 1996).

4.2 Origins
Rubén G. Rumbaut, "Origins and Destinies: Immigration, Race, and Ethnicity in Contemporary America," in *Origins*, above; Michael Fix and Jeffrey S. Passel, with Maria E. Enchautegui and Wendy Zimmerman, *Immigration and Immigrants: Setting the Record Straight* (Urban Institute, May 1994); Schmidley and Gibson, *Profile of the Foreign-Born Population in the United States: 1997*; *Legal Immigration, Fiscal Year 1998*.

4.3 Destinations
U.S. Census Bureau; William H. Frey and Kao-Lee Liaw, "Immigrant Concentration and Domestic Migrant Dispersal: Is Movement to Nonmetropolitian Areas 'White Flight'?" *Professional Geographer* 50(2) (1998): 215–32.

4.4 A Land of Many Tongues
1990 U.S. Census 5% PUMS.

4.5 Diaspora Politics
U.S. Census Bureau; *World Factbook,* CIA, 1999; "New Lithuanian Leader Vows Growth, Cooperation; Former U.S. Official Will Push for Entry to NATO and the EU; Adamkus Succeeds Ex-Communist," *St. Louis Post-Dispatch*, (27 February 1998); Jocelyn Y. Stewart, "Expatriates Have Impact on Mexican Politics," *Los Angeles Times*, (7 May 2000); Juan Forero, "Dominicans Stay Tuned to Voting at Home," *New York Times* (17 May 2000).

4.6 Refugees and Asylum Seekers

Schmidley and Gibson, *Profile of the Foreign-Born Population in the United States: 1997*, U.S. Census Bureau; *Legal Immigration, Fiscal Year 1998*; Leo R. Chavez, "Borders and Bridges: Undocumented Immigrants from Mexico and Central America," in *Origins*, above; Rubén G. Rumbaut, "A Legacy of War," in *Origins*, above.

4.7 Illegal Immigration

David Bacon, "INS Declares War on Labor," *Nation*, (25 December 1999); Immigration and Naturalization Service, "Illegal Alien Resident Population," 1999; Ricardo Romo, "Mexican Americans: Their Civic and Political Incorporation," in *Origins*, above; Chavez, "Borders and Bridges."

4.8 Emigration

Immigration and Naturalization Service, "Immigration Fact Sheet," 2000.

4.9 Getting Through the Door

Fix and Passel, *Immigration and Immigrants; Legal Immigration, Fiscal Year 1998*.

5. Movers

5.1 Imagining the City

U.S. Census Bureau; Gallup 1997; Tim W. Ferguson and William Heuslein, "Best Places," *Forbes* (29 May 2000); Jon Gertner, with Roberta Kirwan, "The Best Places to Live," *Money* (November 1999).

5.2 Contemporary Urban Growth and Demographic Balkanization

William H. Frey, "The New Urban Demographics: Race, Space, and Aging Boomers," *Brookings Review* (Summer 2000); William H. Frey, "Immigration and Demographic Balkanization: Toward One America or Two?" *America's Demographic Tapestry: Baseline from the New Millennium* (New Brunswick, N.J.: Rutgers University Press, 1999).

5.3 Sprawl and Suburban Desire

U.S. Census Bureau.

5.4 Beyond Black Cities and White Suburbs

Frey, "The New Urban Demographics."

5.5 Multiethnic Metros and the Diversity Myth

William H. Frey and Kao-Lee Liaw, "Internal Migration of Foreign-Born Latinos and Asians: Are They Assimilating Geographically?" *Migration and Restructuring in the United States* (New York: Rowman and Littlefield, 1999); William H. Frey, "The Diversity Myth," *American Demographics* (June 1998).

5.6 Today's Domestic Migrant Magnets

Frey, "Immigration and Demographic Balkanization"; William H. Frey, "New Demographic Divide in the U.S.: Immigrant and Domestic Migration 'Migration Magnets', " *Public Perspective* (June/July 1998); William H. Frey and Kao-Lee Liaw, "Immigrant Concentration and Domestic Migrant Dispersal: Is Movement to Nonmetropolitan Areas 'White Flight'?" *Professional Geographer* 50(2) (1998): 215–32.

5.7 The Black Return South

William H. Frey. "Black Migration to the South Reaches Record Highs in the 1990s," *Population Today* (February 1998).

5.8 The Young and the Restless

1990 U.S. Census 5% PUMS.

5.9 Technopolises
Ross De Vol et al., "America's High-Tech Economy: Growth, Development, and Risks for Metropolitan Areas," Milken Institute Research Report, 1999.

5.10 Elderly Movers and Stayers
William H. Frey, "New Sun Belt Metros and Suburbs Are Magnets for Retirees," *Population Today* (October 1999).

6. Classes

6.1 How Americans Classify Themselves
GSS.

6.2 The Rich-Poor Divide
1998 Current Population Survey; U.S. Census Bureau, "Money Income in the United States, 1998," Current Population Reports, series P60–206; Center on Budget and Policy Priorities, "Pulling Apart: A State by State Analysis of Income Trends," December 1997; Randy Albelda and Nancy Folbre, *The War on the Poor: A Defense Manual* (New York: The New Press, 1996).

6.3 Wealth and the Wealthy
Barry W. Johnson, "Personal Wealth, 1995," Internal Revenue Service; poverty data from 1995 Current Population Survey.

6.4 Poverty and Policy
State benefits data are from Stateline.org's resources on welfare reform; long-term trends are from the U.S. Census Bureau; Joseph Dalaker, "Poverty in the U.S.," Current Population Reports (September 1998).

6.5 The Working Poor and the Production of Poverty
Dalaker, "Poverty in the U.S."; Bureau of Labor Statistics.

6.6 Poor Beginnings
U.S. Census Bureau; Dalaker, "Poverty in the U.S."

7. Workers

7.1 Changing Collars
Karl Marx, *The Communist Manifesto*; occupational data from the Integrated Public Use Microdata Set (IPUMS), http://www.ipums.umn.edu/.

7.2 Women at Work
Reynolds Farley, *The New American Reality* (New York: Russell Sage, 1996); graphed data from 1970 and earlier is from *Historical Statistics of the United States, Colonial Times to 1970*, 1975 U.S. Census, data for later years is from the *Statistical Abstract of the United States, 1999*, table no. 653.

7.3 From Field Hands to Harvesters
Farley, *New American Reality*; Randy E. Ilg, "The Changing Face of Farm Employment," *Monthly Labor Review* (April 1995); Jack L. Runyan, "Profile of Hired Farmworkers, 1996 Annual Averages," U.S. Department of Agriculture, Economic Research Service, Food and Rural Economics Division, Agricultural Economic Report no. 762; U.S. Census Bureau, *Statistical Abstract of the United States, 1999*, table 711; graphed data are from Ilg, table 1.

7.4 A Postindustrial Society with Factories

Farley, *New American Reality*; Paul Krugman, *Peddling Prosperity* (New York: W. W. Norton, 1994); map data is from *Statistical Abstract of the United States, 1999*, table 689; data for graph of car production are from *Statistical Abstract of the United States, 1999*, table 1442.

7.5 From Assembly Line to Sales Floor

Farley, *New American Reality*; graphed data are from *Statistical Abstract of the United States, 1999*, table 1432.

7.6 A New Economy?

Anthony Giddens, *Sociology: A Brief but Critical Introduction* (Fort Worth: Harcourt Brace Jovanovich, 1987); Doug Henwood, "Work and Its Future," *Left Business Observer* (April 1996); Joanna Glasner, "Is Your Cubicle Shrinking, Too?" *Wired News* (8 May 2000); occupational projections are from the Bureau of Labor Statistics.

7.7 Fighting for a Piece of the Pie

Bureau of Labor Statistics; Randy Hodson and Teresa A. Sullivan, *The Social Organization of Work* (Belmont, Calif.: Wadsworth, 1990).

7.8 The "Right-to-Work" South

Map data are from *Statistical Abstract of the United States, 1999*, table 720.

8. Families

8.1 Whatever Happened to Marriage?

U.S. Census Bureau, Current Population Reports, series P20–514, "Marital Status and Living Arrangements: March 1998 (Update)"; National Center for Education Statistics, *Youth Indicators 1996*.

8.2 The Mythical Normal Family

U.S. Census Bureau.

8.3 Cohabitation as an Alternative to Marriage

Lynne M. Casper, Philip N. Cohen, and Tavia Simmons, "How Does POSSLQ Measure Up? Historical Estimates of Cohabitation," Population Division Working Paper no. 36, May 1999.

8.4 Single-Parent Households

U.S. Census Bureau, Current Population Reports, series P-20; Steven Ruggles, "The Origins of African American Family Structure," *American Sociological Review* 59 (1994): 136–51.

8.5 Interracial Marriage

U.S. Census Bureau.

8.6 Growing Up Is Different These Days

U.S. Census Bureau, *Statistical Abstract of the United States, 1999*, no. 79.

8.7 Abortion

Alan Guttmacher Institute; *Roe v. Wade*.

8.8 Teen Pregnancy

National Center for Health Statistics, *Health, United States, 1999 with Health and Aging Chartbook*.

9. Students

9.1 Is America Behind?
"International Comparisons of Education," *Digest of Education Statistics 1998*, National Center for Education Statistics; Gerald Bracey, "Are U.S. Students Behind?" *American Prospect* (March–April 1998).
9.2 Staying In, Dropping Out
"High School Dropouts: The Gender Gap," Ameristat, http://www.ameristat.org/edu/dropouts.htm, 2000.
9.3 The Alternatives
Isabel Lyman, "Homeschooling: Back to the Future?" *Cato Policy Analysis* (7 January 1998).
9.4 Minorities and College
Harry P. Pachon, "Perspectives on Affirmative Action: The Real Numbers Offer Nothing to Cheer About; Don't Be Fooled by UC Claims That Discriminatory Measures Haven't Taken a Toll on Enrollment," *Los Angeles Times* (31 January 2000); "Florida Strives for Unity on Affirmative Action," *Atlanta Journal and Constitution* (9 March 2000); William Bowen and Derek Bok, *The Shape of the River* (Princeton, N.J.: Princeton University Press, 1998).
9.5 Enrollment Roller Coaster
"Crowded Classrooms?" Ameristat, http://www.ameristat.org/edu/crowded.htm, 2000.

10. The Elderly

10.2 The Widow Gap
U.S. Census Bureau, *Age 65 and Up in the United States*; American Association of Retired Persons, A *Profile of Older Americans, 1999*.
10.3 The Last White Majority?
U.S. Census Bureau, "Projected Life Expectancy at Birth by Race and Hispanic Origin, 1999 to 2100," table NP-T7-B; U.S. Census Bureau, "Projections of Resident Population, by Age, Sex, and Race: 2000 to 2025," *Statistical Abstract of the United States, 1999*, p. 25, no. 24.
10.4 Elderly Poverty and the Weight of History
U.S. Census Bureau, "Educational Attainment, by Sex: 1910 to 1998," *Statistical Abstract of the United States, 1999*, p. 877, no. 1426; "Historical Poverty Tables: People," http://www.census.gov/hhes/poverty/histpov/phtpov3.html (31 May 2000).
10.5 From Work to Retirement and Back
Henry Aaron, "The Centarian Boom," *Brookings Review* 18 (2) (Spring 2000); U.S. Census Bureau, *Age 65 and Up in the United States*; Murray Gendell and Jacob S. Segel, "Trends in Retirement Age by Sex, 1950–2005," *Monthly Labor Review* (July 1992): 22–29.
10.6 Where the Boomers Will Retire
U.S. Census Bureau; William H. Frey, "New Sun Belt Metros and Suburbs Are Magnets for Retirees," *Population Today* (October 1999).
10.7 How to Stay Healthy
U.S. Census Bureau, *Age 65 and Up in the United States*; American Association of Retired Persons, *A Profile of Older Americans, 1999*; *Statistical Abstract of the United States, 1999*, p. 875, no. 1422.

10.8 Neglected Violence
Administration on Aging, *The National Elder Abuse Incidence Study*, September 1998; National Center on Elder Abuse, *Elder Abuse Information Series No. 2*; U.S. Census Bureau, "Cancer—Estimated 1980–82 to 1989–95," *Statistical Abstract of the United States, 1999*, p. 154, no. 241.

11. The Healthy

11.1 American Lives
National Center for Health Statistics, "New Healthy Life Expectancy Rankings: Japan #1 in New 'Healthy Life' System," *WHO Issues: Health, United States, 1999 with Health and Aging Chartbook*; *Projected Life Expectancy at Birth, 1999*, Middle Series, National Projections Program; U.S. Census Bureau.
11.2 Medicine's Charge
Microsoft Encarta Reference Suite 2000; *Encyclopedia Britannica*.
11.3 Infant Mortality
Historical Statistical Abstracts of the United States from Colonial Times to the Present; National Center for Health Statistics; *Health, United States, 1999 with Health and Aging Chartbook*.
11.4 The Demography of Destiny
WellWeb.com, "Sickle-Cell Anemia;" Federation of American Societies for Experimental Biology, "Policy Statement: American College of Medical Genetics Fragile X Syndrome: Diagnostic & Carrier Testing"; March of Dimes, "Tay-Sachs Disease Public Health Education Information Sheet"; Muscular Dystrophy Association, "Facts about Muscular Dystrophy."
11.5 People with AIDS
U.S. Census Bureau, *Statistical Abstract of the United States, 1999*.
11.6 The Uninsured
U.S. Census Bureau, *Health Insurance Coverage, 1998*.
11.7 Smoking
National Center for Health Statistics; Gallup, 1998; *Health, United States, 1999 with Health and Aging Chartbook*; Dr. Marie Swanson, "Today, Take a Moment to Recall Why Smoking Stinks," *Detroit Free Press* (19 November 1998).
11.8 Disabled America
U.S. Census Bureau, *Statistical Abstract of the United States, 1999*.
11.9 Evading Death
"Death Rate for Selected Causes: 1900–1970," *Historical Statistical Abstracts of the United States from Colonial Times to the Present*, series B, 149–66; National Center for Health Statistics, *Health, United States, 1999 with Health and Aging Chartbook*.

12. Criminals

12.1 Guns and the American Dream
Encyclopedia Britannica; "Arms and the Man," *Economist*, U.S. ed. (3 July 1999).
12.2 America the Violent?

The Fifth United Nations Survey of Crime Trends and Operations of Criminal Justice Systems (1990–1994); International Data Base, U.S. Census Bureau.

12.3 Murder Rates Vary by Region
Bureau of Justice Statistics, Sourcebook of Criminal Justice Statistics 1998; Richard E. Nisbett and Dov Cohen, Culture of Honor: The Psychology of Violence in the South (Boulder, Colo.: Westview, 1996).

12.4 But Things Aren't Getting Worse
Bureau of Justice Statistics; National Center for Health Statistics.

12.5 An Eye for an Eye
Fox Butterfield, "Death Sentences Being Overturned in 2 of 3 Appeals," New York Times, (12 June 2000); Bureau of Justice Statistics, Capital Punishment, 1997.

12.6 The Prison Boom
Bureau of Justice Statistics, "Correctional Populations in the United States, 1980–96"; Steven R. Donziger, ed., The Real War on Crime: The Report of the National Criminal Justice Commission (New York: HarperPerennial, 1996); "Stateline: Competing with Russia for Prison Numbers," State Legislatures 25 (8) (September 1999); Bureau of Justice Statistics, "Justice Expenditure and Employment in the United States, 1995."

12.7 Punishment
Christopher Uggen and Jeff Manza, "The Political Consequences of Felon Disenfranchisement Laws in the United States," unpublished working paper, 2000; Andrew L. Shapiro, "Challenging Criminal Disenfranchisement under the Voting Rights Act: A New Strategy," Yale Law Journal (November 1993).

12.8 Justice and the Color Line
1996 U.S. Census; Bureau of Justice Statistics, Correctional Populations in the United States, 1996; Bureau of Justice Statistics, Capital Punishment, 1996; Jesse Jackson, Legal Lynching: Racism, Injustice, and the Death Penalty (New York: Marlowe, 1996).

12.9 Prisons as Factories
Data for 1992: Bureau of Labor Statistics; annual report of Federal Prison Industries, Inc. (Unicor); Gordon Lafer, "Captive Labor: America's Prisoners as Corporate Workforce," American Prospect (September–October 1999).

12.10 Violence Against Women
Bureau of Justice Statistics.

12.11 The Violence of Hate
Southern Poverty Law Center; Federal Bureau of Investigation, Hate Crime Statistics, 1998; Bureau of Justice Statistics, U.S. Department of Justice, 1997.

13. Voters

13.1 The Making of the American Electorate
Eric Foner, The Story of American Freedom (New York: W. W. Norton, 1998); Laughlin Macdonald, "Voting in the United States: It Wasn't Always for Everybody," American Civil Liberties Union; Encyclopedia Britannica; Andrew L. Shapiro, "Challenging Criminal Disenfranchise-

ment under the Voting Rights Act: A New Strategy," *Yale Law Journal* (November 1993).

13.2 Who Are the Democrats?

Pew Research Center for the People and the Press, *RETRO-POLITICS: The Political Typology: Version 3.0*, November 1999; Pew Research Center for the People and the Press, *DEMOCRATS: A Demographic and Attitudinal Profile (Tables Only)*, August, 1996; Michael Omi and Howard Winant, *Racial Formation in the United States* (New York: Routledge, 1994).

13.3 Who Are the Republicans?

Pew Research, *RETRO-POLITICS;* Pew Research, *DEMOCRATS;* Omi and Winant, *Racial Formation in the United States*.

13.4 Who Remains Independent?

Pew Research, *RETRO-POLITICS*; Pew Research, *DEMOCRATS*.

13.5 Are We Growing Apart?

U.S. Census Bureau, *Voting and Registration in the Election of November 1996 (Detailed Tables)*; Pew Research, *DEMOCRATS*; Julie Kosterlitz, "Boomers, Say Hola," *National Journal* 31 (33): 2362.

13.6 90210 and the Buying of the Presidency

"White Gold: The Zip Codes That Matter Most to the Presidential Candidates," *Public Campaign* (December 1999); Center for Responsive Politics, "Who Paid for This Election?"

13.7 Voter Apathy

Marshall Ganz, "Voters in the Crosshairs: How Technology and the Market Are Destroying Politics," *American Prospect*, no. 16 (Winter 1994); Robert Dreyfuss, "The Turnout Imperative," *American Prospect*, no. 39 (July–August 1998).

13.8 Class Participation: Grade: F

U.S. Census Bureau, *Voting and Registration in the Election of 1996*.